NEWMAN FOR OUR TIME

Msgr. Larry Spiteri

NEWMAN FOR OUR TIME

Saint, Scholar, and Doctor of the Church

Foreword by Cardinal Pietro Parolin

SOPHIA INSTITUTE PRESS
Manchester, New Hampshire

Cover by LUCAS Art & Design, Jenison, MI

Cover image: Photo of John Henry Newman (Wikimedia Commons)

Sophia Institute Press

Box 5284, Manchester, NH 03108

1-800-888-9344

www.SophiaInstitute.com

Sophia Institute Press is a registered trademark of Sophia Institute.

paperback ISBN 979-8-88911-592-2

ebook ISBN 979-8-88911-593-9

Library of Congress Control Number: 2025946768

First printing

Contents

Foreword

St. John Henry Newman chose for his motto as a cardinal *Cor ad cor loquitur*, "Heart speaks to heart." The motto reflects the lively and constant dialogue that took place between the Heart of God and the heart of the sainted cardinal. It reminds us also of St. Teresa of Ávila, a Doctor of the Church, who understood prayer as a heart-to-heart conversation with Him who loves us (see *Catechism of the Catholic Church*, 2709). In the case of Newman, this was more than an exclusive exchange between himself and God, for his heart was also able to speak to other people's desire for a personal relationship with the Lord.

In this sense, Cardinal Newman continues to speak to us who live more than a century after his death on August 11, 1890. We see this in the substantial literature devoted to his writings by both Catholic and non-Catholic theologians and scholars. Indeed, today Newman is probably better known for his outstanding sermons and writings than for his other accomplishments.

An impressive number of episcopal conferences worldwide, as well as clergy, scholars, and institutions, both Catholic and non-Catholic, attest to the fact that Newman continues to exercise great influence in the fields of theology and ecumenism. He is frequently referred to as a precursor of the Second Vatican Council and a silent presence and inspiration in such areas as the development of doctrine, the dialogue between magisterium and theology, and the interplay between Scripture, Tradition, and the Fathers — to say nothing of the relationship between faith and reason, the role of the laity, the primacy of conscience, moral theology, ecclesiology, and education. His celebrated sermons as an Anglican minister and then as a Catholic priest reveal his deep learning and his mastery of both the spoken and the written word.

Many Popes since Leo XIII have appealed to Newman's writings and acute insights. Pope Leo XIII honored Newman by creating him a cardinal in the consistory of May 12, 1879, and appointing him cardinal deacon of San Giorgio in Velabro the following May 15. Pope Benedict XVI especially admired his writings and considered it a great personal privilege to beatify him on September 19, 2010, during his apostolic journey to England.

In this present work, Msgr. Laurence J. Spiteri attentively weaves a tapestry uniting Cardinal Newman's personal life and his outstanding teachings. He shows how the "kindly light" that guided Newman throughout his life led him to give up his prominent position as a renowned and well-respected Anglican to join the Church of Rome. His spiritual journey was marked by many obstacles, criticisms, misunderstandings, false accusations, public and private disparagement, and heartrending separation from close friends. Yet, as a man completely committed to the search for the truth, he never failed to be guided by that "kindly light" in his vast research and profound scholarship. His long and eventful life was constantly inspired by his intimate relationship with the Lord, which was best expressed by those words: *Cor ad cor loquitur.*

Cardinal Pietro Parolin
Secretary of State of His Holiness
Vatican City

PREFACE

I WAS GREATLY SURPRISED and humbled when the Catholic hierarchy of England and Wales appointed me to serve as the first postulator for the theological and canonical (legal) argument to have the Holy Father Pope Francis declare Cardinal St. John Henry Newman a *Doctor of the Church* for his eminent teaching. The postulator is assisted by a number of experts in the life and writings of the candidate. One of the assistants is an Anglican priest in this instance, indicating clearly that the saint is an inspiration to non-Roman Catholics as well.

I have been a great admirer of St. John Henry Newman (1801–1890) since my days in Oxford, England, when I was a very young student. I felt his presence every time I visited the Anglican University Church of St. Mary the Virgin. It was here that he delivered some of his greatest homilies while he was still an Anglican priest, and very proud to be so.

Today we claim this saint as one of our very own — a Catholic priest, Oratorian, cardinal, and the newest Doctor of the Catholic Church. A title bestowed by a Roman Pontiff on saints who are recognized as having made a significant contribution to theology or doctrine through their research, study, or writing, or a combination of these areas.

Prior to Newman, the Catholic Church named thirty-seven Doctors of the Universal Church. Twenty-eight of these declared Doctors are from the Western Church and nine from the Eastern Catholic Churches. There are four women and thirty-three men. They are a mixture of saintly persons. One is an abbess, three are nuns, and one is a tertiary associated with a religious order. Two Doctors are Popes, nineteen are bishops, twelve are priests, and one is a deacon. Twenty-seven are Europeans, three are Africans, and seven are from Asia. Chronologically, the largest fraction of them, twelve in total, lived during the fourth century. Eminent Catholic writers of the first, second, and third centuries are usually referred to as the Ante-Nicene Fathers; that is, they lived before the First Council of Nicaea in A.D. 325.

To date, St. Alphonsus Liguori (1696–1787), a bishop and the founder of the Redemptorist congregation, experienced the shortest period between his death (1787) and his declaration as Doctor of the Church (1871), a span of just eighty-four years. The longest period between death and declaration was the bishop-martyr St. Irenaeus of Lyon, who was born in 130 and martyred between 200 and 203. Pope Francis declared St. Irenaeus the thirty-seventh Doctor of the Church on January 21, 2022—some eighteen centuries after he was martyred. He is also the most recently recognized Doctor of the Church.

In the Western (Latin) side of the Catholic Church, since the eighth century, four saints had been given a special, preeminent position for their theology. They are St. Ambrose (339–397), St. Augustine (354–430), St. Jerome (347–420), and Pope Gregory the Great (ca. 540–604). They were declared Great Doctors of the Church in 1298 by Pope Boniface VIII (reigned 1294–1303). On the other hand, Pope Pius V (reigned 1566–1572) recognized the four Great Doctors of the Eastern Catholic Churches in 1568, right after the Council of Trent (1545–1563) and in the midst of the Catholic Counter-Reformation. They are St. John Chrysostom (ca. 347–407), St. Basil the Great (330–379), St. Gregory of Nazianzus (329–390), and St. Athanasius of Alexandria (296–373).

John Henry Newman was a brilliant scholar in search of the Truth and the true Church. Though we claim him as our own, so does the Anglican Church from which he set forth on his long search, which ended with him converting to Roman Catholicism. His long journey was full of trials, disillusionments, sorrow, crises, sheer intellectual honesty, and heartaches. He persevered. The Lord in due course bestowed upon him the gift of the Roman Catholic Faith. His conversion was not exactly what one would call easy, popular, and devoid of hurdles. Yet, while there was inner and outward turmoil, he never gave up and called it quits because his conversion journey was becoming more and more controversial and touched directly his soul and public life. He was led by that "gentle light" which he wrote about.

The aim of this book is to assist its reader to understand better the laborious journey of this new Doctor of the Church and to present his exceptional theological contribution as both an Anglican divine and a Roman Catholic priest. May he pray for us as we pray through his intercession!

Msgr. Laurence J. Spiteri,
Vatican City

NEWMAN FOR OUR TIME

ONE

John Henry Newman as Member of the Church of England

Many of us have heard about and are aware of King Henry VIII of England (reigned 1509–1547) for two main reasons: his multiple marriages — six in all, entailing the beheading of two of his queens (Anne Boleyn and Catherine Howard); and having himself declared the earthly supreme head of the Church of England, thus creating a national English Church separated from the Roman Catholic Church. When his petition to Pope Clement VII (reigned 1523–1534) failed to procure an annulment of his (first) marriage to Queen Catherine of Aragon (1485–1536), he established his own church. The English Parliament passed the Act of Supremacy in 1534, recognizing by law that Henry VIII was the supreme head on earth of the Church of England, thereby legally severing all ecclesiastical links to Rome and the Pope. He procured from the new church authorities, under Thomas Cranmer (1489–1556) — the first Protestant Archbishop of Canterbury — the annulment of his marriage so that he could marry his pregnant lover, Anne Boleyn (ca. 1507–1536), wrongly believing that she would provide him with the longed-for son and future successor on the throne.

Henry embarked on persecuting every person who opposed his new religion program, called the English Reformation. The most notable victims among the 430 martyrs from 1534 to 1544 were St. Thomas More (1478–1535) — his former intimate friend and lord chancellor—and Bishop St. John Fisher of Rochester (1469–1535). Thomas More was renowned for his legal and theological scholarship, deep religious observance, great sense of justice, piercing wit, and total allegiance to the papacy. Fisher, meanwhile, had been a tutor to the young Henry. He was also the confessor of Henry VIII's grandmother, Margaret Beaufort, Countess of Richmond and Derby and mother of Henry VIII's father, the first Tudor king, Henry VII (reigned 1485–1509). Fisher was held prisoner in the Tower of London for publicly supporting the marriage between Henry and Catherine (thereby stressing the indissolubility of marriage), refusing to take the oath which declared Anne Boleyn's issue as the legitimate heirs to the English throne, rejecting the title of the king as Supreme Head of the Church of England, and upholding papal supremacy. Ironically, both of these martyrs are listed today as saints in the Calendar of Saints in the Church of England.

The Church of England has undergone several developments and subdivisions over the centuries, though consistently holding that the sacraments of Baptism and Eucharist were necessary for salvation. However, while the sacrament of Baptism was deemed valid by the Catholic Church, Pope Leo XIII (reigned 1878–1903), in his apostolic letter entitled *Apostolicae curae,* issued on September 13, 1896, declared that all Anglican ordinations (deacon, priest, and bishop) were invalid because he found the Anglican Edwardine Ordinals deficient in intention and form, thereby breaking apostolic succession. The Edwardine Ordinals were two liturgical books written primarily by Thomas Cranmer. The first was published in 1550 and the second in 1552. They are called "Edwardine" because the rite was established by King Edward VI (reigned 1547–1553). Thus, the Roman Catholic Church, as a direct consequence of maintaining the invalidity of Anglican orders, also rendered invalid the Anglican Eucharist.

The community of Evangelicals was diffuse at the time of Newman. The movement had distant roots in the Protestant Puritans that mushroomed toward the last years of Queen Elizabeth I (reigned 1558–1603) and gloried in the Commonwealth and Free State of England established by Oliver Cromwell (ruled 1653–1658) in May 1649, which suppressed the English monarchy for more than a decade. The new way of ruling England was extinguished by the restoration of the monarchy with Charles II (reigned 1660–1685) in 1660.

The Evangelical version of Christianity had a comeback in the eighteenth century, when it produced the dissident Methodist Church. Its members deemed themselves as the spiritual, fervent, unworldly branch within the Anglican Church. They stressed affections and emotions. This was the Christian group to which belonged Thomas Scott and William Romaine, both of whom influenced the young John Henry Newman. Later, Newman referred to the Evangelicals in Oxford as "Protestant" or "Ultra Protestant." While the Evangelicals denied the doctrine of baptismal regeneration, the Methodists claimed that the visible English Church had many nominal Christians and that the true church comprised only those who were saved.

Fr. Newman's main clash was with liberal Anglicans at Oxford. They practically ran him out of the university and the city. This religious group viewed Christianity as part of a broader understanding of truth, deeming it to be fluid. They became prominent in Oxford in the 1860s. Many members belonged to the educated class. Newman maintained that their fundamental principle was that dogma was an opinion and nothing was objectively true; therefore, nothing was permanent. This meant that there was no problem whatsoever with any kind of religious opinions.

In order to understand how Newman's attitude developed, we have to look at his upbringing and education. He was born on Old

Broad Street in London on February 21, 1801, at his parental home at 17 Southampton Place. Today the place is marked by a blue plaque on the visitors' entrance to the London Stock Exchange. He was baptized on April 9, 1801, in the Church of St. Benet Fink.

He was the eldest of six children, three boys and three girls.[1] His parents, John Newman and Jemima Fourdrinier, were married on September 24, 1799, in St. Mary's Parish Church in Lambert. The war between England and the brutal Revolutionary French regime had been raging since 1793 and it would last until 1802. At the time of the Newman marriage, England was in deep national crisis due to British and Russian defeat by the French-Dutch army at the Battle of Bergen-Binnen on September 19, 1899.

The Newmans were married about six weeks before Napoleon Bonaparte (1769–1821) successfully staged his coup d'état in France on November 9–10, 1799, abolishing the ruling corrupt French Directory and appointing himself as France's First Consul, marking the end of the bloody French Revolution (1789–1799) and ushering in the controversial Napoleonic era on November 9, 1799. England was still at war when baby John Henry was born.

Newman's father, John, was an honest conventional banker. His ancestry could be traced back to at least the seventeenth century. Jemima Fourdrinier was the daughter of a prosperous paper merchant of Huguenot origins. Her Huguenot ancestors had fled France to England after King Louis XIV (reigned 1643–1715) revoked the Edict of Nantes on October 18, 1685. The Newman family was a happy one.

It has often been said that the Newman family was Evangelical. In fact, it belonged to the Church of England, though by no means was it

[1] His siblings were Charles (b. June 16, 1802), Harriett (b. December 10, 1803), Francis (b. June 27, 1805), Jemima (b. May 19, 1808), and Mary (b. November 9, 1809).

very religious in practice. However, as was customary at the time, young Newman read the Bible and had a perfect knowledge of his catechism.[2] He showed signs of mental precociousness at a young age.

The small boy Newman was enlisted as a pupil at Great Ealing School at age seven. He showed no real interest in any kind of athletics, but exhibited strong leadership in the Boys Club. He was an avid reader of poems and of the novels of Sir Walter Scott and Robert Southey. He read the skeptical works of Thomas Paine and David Hume when he was fourteen. It was during this very early youth that he indicated clear signs of being a very promising writer.

The year 1816 was an eventful one for the teenage Newman. The end of the Napoleonic Wars (1803–1815) was followed by substantial inflation in England. The bank of Newman's father failed in 1816. Next, the Newman family settled in Alton, but the older Newman's attempt to manage a brewery was unsuccessful. The young John Henry, now age fifteen, stayed at Great Ealing School for that summer. It was his last year at that school. It also was during this time that he fell ill, the first of three major illnesses, each of which was accompanied by intense spiritual experiences.

The young Newman matriculated on December 14, 1816, at Trinity College, Oxford, but did not take up residence until the following June (1817). College living was a new world for the teenager. He was about three years younger than his classmates, many of whom bullied him to get drunk. He resisted their attempts and spent endless hours in studying. He soon became a close friend of John William Bowden (1798–1844).

The fifteen-year-old Newman, in 1816, had been lent some books in the English Calvinist tradition by Reverend Walter Mayers

2 John Henry Newman, *Apologia Pro Vita Sua* (Longman, Green, Longman, Roberts, and Green 1864), chap. 5.

(1790–1882). Mayers was a master at the school, and Newman's spiritual advisor at the time. This literature played a role in Newman's eventual conversion to Calvinistic Christianity, which he would discover later fell outside the practices of Evangelical Christianity. This commitment lasted five months, from August to December 1816. Arthur Wollaston Hutton relates, "It was in the autumn of 1816 that Newman fell under the influence of a definite creed and received into his intellect impressions of dogma never afterwards effaced."[3] Influenced by the writings of Thomas Newman (no relation), John Henry became a typical Evangelical Calvinist who asserted that the Pope was the antichrist.[4]

The classical process in Evangelical Christianity was an intellectual conversion, giving certitude of the existence of God and the soul's relationship to God. Newman joined this brand of Christianity at the end of 1816. When Newman was in his sunset years, he looked back at his conversion to Evangelical Christianity in 1816 as the saving of his soul, as he began to move away from Calvinism. Eamon Duffy comments that Newman "came to see Evangelicalism, with its emphasis on religious feeling and on the Reformation doctrine of justification by faith alone, as a Trojan horse for an undogmatic religious individualism that ignored the Church's role in the transmission of revealed truth, and that must lead inexorably to subjectivism and skepticism."[5]

He recalled the event of this conversion in his *Apologia Pro Vita Sua*, stating,

[3] Arthur Wollaston Hutton, "Newman, John Henry," in *Encyclopedia Britannica*, 11th ed., vol. 19, ed. Hugh Chisholm (Cambridge University Press, 1911), 517.

[4] Sheridan Gilley, *Newman and His Age* (Darton, Longman, and Todd, 2003), 31.

[5] Eamon Duffy, "A Hero of the Church," *New York Times Review of Books*, December 23, 2010.

> When I was fifteen a great change of thought took place in me. I fell under the influences of a definite Creed.... I believed that the inward conversion of which I was conscious ... would last into the next life, and that I was elected to eternal glory.... I believe that it had some influence on my opinions ... in isolating me from the objects which surrounded me, in confirming me in my mistrust of the reality of material phenomena, and making me rest in the thought of two and two only absolute and luminously self-evident beings, myself and my creator ... more certain than that I have hands or feet.[6]

He later would refer to this as being his first conversion.

However, it was the writings of the English Evangelical divine Joseph Milner (1744–1797) that got the young Newman deeply interested in the Fathers of the Church, as he read Milner's *History of the Church of Christ*.[7] The Fathers' teachings would play a major role in Newman's quest for the true Church and in identifying her as being the Roman Catholic Church.

The young Newman won a nine-year Oxford University Trinity College scholarship in May 1818 at age seventeen. Next, following a short stint at Lincoln's Inn in London, he returned to Trinity College on February 12, 1821. The following summer he began summarizing on paper his Evangelical beliefs, as found in his *Private Journal*. He finished the summary in the early months of 1822. He was surprised to realize that his conversion was not consistent with the description of conversion set by Evangelical writers. Newman's *Private Journal*

6 Newman, *Apologia Pro Vita Sua*, chap. 1.

7 This work is composed of five volumes. The first three volumes were written by Joseph Milner, while the last two volumes were written by his brother Isaac Milner.

revealed his serious undertaking to lead a spiritual life and to overcome what he considered his main mistakes and sins, especially pride, vanity, ambition, anger, pugnacity, ill-temper, and sexual thoughts, as well as his efforts to turn away from them. Meanwhile his mother thought he was becoming self-righteous to the point of being zealous, while his father became increasingly irritated with his son's fervent Evangelical adherence. His father finally lost his temper and told him, on January 11, 1822, to make up his mind about what he wanted to be. The young Newman opted for the Church of England. He returned to Oxford the following day to prepare for the prestigious Oriel College Fellowship examination. But he academically failed to shine in his examination, graduating with a bachelor of arts, with lower second-class honors in classics. Nonetheless, Newman wanted to remain in Oxford and, thus, he took up privately tutoring some students. He was subsequently elected as a fellow at Oriel College on April 12, 1822, at age twenty-one. This college was the recognized center of Oxford intellectual life.

Newman postposed taking up residence at Oriel for four years. Upon arriving, he discovered a world very alien to him. He felt intimidated by his colleagues, was self-conscious, and sensed spiritual isolation. The fellows wondered if they had made a mistake in electing him. So they entrusted him to Richard Whately, who concluded that the choice was absolutely correct.

Newman befriended a number of persons at Oriel. Some of these would play a significant role in his future ministry as a member of the Anglican clergy. One of them was Edward Bouverie Pusey (1800–1882). They met during the spring of 1823 and soon developed a spiritual bond. Eventually Pusey would become an Anglican priest and the virtual founder and one of the leaders of the Oxford Movement, with special interest in sacramental theology and Sacred Scripture. He was the ideal person for the latter because he served as

Regius Professor of Hebrew at the university for more than fifty years (1828–1882).

Newman began his life as an Anglican minister when he was ordained a deacon of the Anglican Church on June 13, 1824, at Christ Church Cathedral, Oxford. He prepared himself for his ordination by fasting — something unusual in the contemporary Church of England. He was overwhelmed when he vowed responsibility for the souls entrusted to him until death, and he was resolute to uphold it. He never lost sight of this vow, as substantiated by his ministry while a member of the Anglican clergy and then the Roman Catholic priesthood.

Newman was ordained a priest by Bishop Edward Legge of Oxford on May 29, 1825, in the same cathedral. At the suggestion of his friend Edward Bouverie Pusey, he served at St. Clement Church in Oxford for the next two years.

Newman had begun his preaching career on June 23, 1824, while still a deacon. His first homily was the seed from which would emerge his genius as a preacher. However, his zealous pastoral work during his two years at St. Clement (1824–1826) went generally unnoticed. He visited the house of every one of his parishioners. He instituted a census in his parish and added a second sermon on Sundays. He was very close to sick parishioners, whom he visited on a regular basis, and took great interest in their spiritual well-being. He aimed his ministry, including his preaching, at helping people become holy. His sermons, in which he presented most of his theological teachings, touched on the necessity of living an authentic Christian life and not merely one which renders lip service; every person's call to holiness; the importance of studying Sacred Scripture; the need to repent and reject worldly values since everyone is a sinner; and the benefits of frequent (Anglican) communion. In other words, he was a dedicated Anglican clergyman.

The young deacon lost his father on October 3, 1824, soon after he began his ministry at St. Clement. Being the oldest child and son, John Henry assumed responsibility for his widowed mother and sisters. He remained very busy in the parish, but also in other institutions. He was elected junior treasurer at Oriel College the following October 15 and became vice principal of St. Alban's Hall on March 26, 1825. Part of his duties was to lecture, an exercise that was one of his fortes.

He was deeply saddened by the death of his grandmother in May 1825, right before his ordination as an Anglican priest. She was his early benefactor and also prompted him to fall into lasting love with Sacred Scripture.

After his priestly ordination, Newman returned to Oriel College in January 1826 in the capacity of tutor. He resigned his position at St. Clement the following February 21, so as to dedicate himself to his role as tutor, viewing it not merely as a secular office but also as one which required a pastoral and religious attentiveness. He saw his purpose as gaining souls for God and was determined to do so. He cultivated friendship and closeness with his students, succeeding in having a religious effect on them. This spiritual hold would increase with the passage of time. It would, in fact, become a threat in Oxford.

He and his friend Richard Hurrell Froude (1803–1836) formed and promoted a high ideal of the tutorial office, emphasizing that it was more clerical and pastoral than secular, thereby laying the foundation of a new character for the office of tutor. This led to serious tensions within the college.

Newman was appointed preacher at Whitehall in 1827.[8] During that summer, apart from tutoring, he was reading about seven to eight hours a day to prepare himself for the role of public examiner

[8] Hutton, "Newman," 517.

for the upcoming academic term. He noticed, to his great personal distress, that he was beginning to prefer intellectual excellence to moral excellence.[9] He had to remind himself of his pastoral mission.

Next, he experienced his second major illness. He collapsed on November 26, 1827, while evaluating a school. He was forced to take a rest and to take better care of his health. The next blow came on January 5, 1828, when his youngest sister, Mary, died at the age of eighteen. Both his second major illness and the death of his young sister had major spiritual effects on his life: he detached himself more from the world and felt more assured that he was on the road to perfection. He felt God's hand in both sad events, guiding him away from worldly aspirations and promises. Furthermore, there was another personal loss, which reminded him of the ephemeral nature of the promises and glory of a passing world. His friend and mentor Walter Mayers died on February 22, 1828.

Newman was appointed vicar to the Oxford University Church of St. Mary the Virgin on March 14, 1828. He described this appointment as a spring after a winter.[10]

Though still associated with the Evangelicals, Newman's views began to gradually assume a higher ecclesiastical tone. In the middle of 1828, he began attentively reading the Church Fathers, which, unknowingly to him at the time, proved to be the first step toward Roman Catholicism.

Sometime during the beginning of 1829, Newman, Robert Wilberforce (1802–1857), and Richard Hurrell Froude, tutor colleagues, enacted a modification of the tutorial system of lectures which provided them with greater control over their own students. The dean allowed this on a trial basis, but when Edward Hawkins

[9] Newman, *Apologia Pro Vita Sua,* 14.

[10] Ibid., 16.

(1789–1882), Oriel's provost, heard of it, he became furious and ordered the three tutors to cease and desist and to immediately revert to the old system. Since all three refused, Hawkins did not assign them any more students. Newman stated that his refusal was based on the principle of following his conscience, and that he was willing to resign as tutor if he was not allowed to fulfill the pastoral and instructional obligations of his office. Reflecting back on this episode, Newman saw the hand of Divine Providence, for the Tractarian Movement would have never come to be, had he not been deprived of his tutorship.[11] Another positive outcome of this event was that he now had enough free time to focus on the Fathers of the Church and to compose his first book, *The Arians of the Fourth Century.*

In 1831, Newman became the select preacher at Oxford University from which he would resign the following year. He was invited in March 1831 to write a history of the First Council of Nicaea (325). However, in the process of doing so, his mind wandered back to the history before that Council (called *ante-Nicene*) and then to the Church of Alexandria. This produced a mature expression of his ideas and influenced his spiritual journey. He resumed working on his book in the making, *The Arians of the Fourth Century.* However, he became completely exhausted by the end of June 1832. He needed some serious time to rest. So, he accepted the invitation of his friend Froude to join him and his father on a tour of the Mediterranean. He preached his last university homily on December 2, 1832. Seven years would pass before he resumed preaching. This time span indicated the mounting anxiety and resistance at the university concerning his growing influence.

[11] Henry Tristram, ed. *John Henry Newman: Autobiographical Writings* (Sheed and Ward, 1956), 96.

The Froudes and Newman set out on a tour of the Mediterranean during December 1832. They visited Gibraltar, Malta, the Ionian Islands, Sicily, Naples, and Rome. At the time, Italy was still a divided peninsula, not yet united into one country. Sicily and Naples formed the Kingdom of the Two Sicilies, which lasted until 1861, when Francis II (1836–1894), the last Bourbon king of Naples and Sicily, was deposed by King Emmanuel II (1820–1878), who joined it to his Kingdom of Piedmont-Sardinia. Victor Emmanuel II was declared king of Italy on March 17, 1861. At the time Rome, governed by Blessed Pius IX (reigned 1846–1878), was under French protection. The new Italian king took advantage of the opportunity to conquer the Papal States after the French withdrew from Rome during the Franco-Prussian War (1870). He entered Rome on September 20, 1870. He declared the city the new capital of Italy on February 3, 1871. The First Vatican Council (1869–1870) was in session at the time of the capture of Rome. Pope Pius IX suspended the Council and declared himself "prisoner of the Vatican."

Now, back to Newman's Mediterranean tour. He reached Rome in 1833. He described the Roman Catholic Church as "polytheistic, degrading and idolatrous." Of course, he would later refute this description.

When the Froudes left to return home overland, Newman decided to return to Sicily with an assistant by the name of Gennaro. He set out for Messina on April 22, but the journey sorely taxed his health. He became deadly ill with a high fever. This turned out to be his third major illness — and perhaps the most intense of the three spiritual experiences associated with his diverse illnesses. Gennaro thought that Newman was dying, but Newman assured him that it was not his time. After three days in his sick bed at Leonforte, Newman thought that he had recovered enough to be able to continue with the journey, only to collapse after covering just seven miles. He stayed at Castro Giovanni for the next three weeks under a highly competent doctor's care. By now Newman was convinced that God had preserved his life because He had a project for him to carry out in England. He saw this assignment as the reformation of the Church of England and its defense against the liberalism then raging in his homeland, not only in civil society but also within his church.

On May 25, Newman set out in a carriage for Palermo, where he stayed until June 13. Meanwhile, he was regaining his strength. He finally left on a small ship heading for Marseilles. But the ship was temporarily stuck in the Straits of Bonifacio, between Corsica and Sardinia. It was during this tour that Newman showed his poetic talents by writing most of his short poems, and it was on this ship that he wrote his famous poem, "Lead, Kindly Light":[12]

> Lead, Kindly Light, amidst th'encircling gloom,
> Lead Thou me on!
> The night is dark, and I am far from home,
> Lead Thou me on!
> Keep Thou my feet; I do not ask to see
> The distant scene; one step enough for me.
>
> I was not ever thus, nor prayed that Thou
> Shouldst lead me on;
> I loved to choose and see my path; but now
> Lead Thou me on!
> I loved the garish day, and, spite of fears,
> Pride ruled my will. Remember not past years!
> So long Thy power hath blessed me, sure it still

[12] "Lead, Kindly Light" later became a popular hymn, though Newman constantly insisted it was just a poem.

Will lead me on.
O'er moor and fen, o'er crag and torrent, till
The night is gone,
And with the morn those angel faces smile,
Which I have loved long since, and lost awhile!

It is this "light" which would inspire and guide Newman for the rest of his life.

By now, Newman was sincerely repentant of his self-will and determined to joyfully surrender to God's will. He sensed that he was entering a new phase in his spiritual journey. Later, while still living in Oxford, Newman deemed his serious third illness as a crucial and providential crisis in his life. He was completely transformed spiritually, recommitting himself to seek holiness by discovering God's will, to be faithful to the light that he had received from on high, and to energetically detach himself from worldly allurements and ambitions by putting his total trust in God's providence. This inner transformation was based on his conviction that he had received a divine light that would sustain him amidst trials, adversities, misunderstandings, controversies, and anxieties. In a way, Newman could have quoted St. Paul's Letter to the Galatians: "Have I now become your enemy by telling you the truth?" (Gal. 4:16).

Once Newman was back in Oxford on July 9, 1833, he undertook his "Mission in England," zealously defending the Church of England against liberalism. He became deeply involved in the materializing Oxford Movement and soon was perceived as its leader. It all began when John Keble (1792–1866) preached at St. Mary's on "National Apostasy" in his Assize Sermon in Oxford on July 14, 1833. Newman regarded the sermon to be the initiation of the Oxford Movement. Keble repudiated the British Parliament's authority to suppress several Anglican dioceses in Ireland. Edward Pusey, John Henry Newman, and John Keble, in particular, feared that the Church of England was in danger of apostasy, and they became convinced that it had abandoned its heritage as a catholic and apostolic church. This conviction led these three, along with others of the same mind, to begin publishing a series of pamphlets known as *Tracts for the Times,* which beckoned the Church of England to return to the former ways, becoming a church undivided in matters of doctrine, liturgy, and devotion. Though the authors strongly opposed the abuses they perceived as being present in the Roman Catholic Church, nevertheless, they were labeled "papists" and rejected by many, although others were convinced by the contents of the *Tracts*.

People in general referred to the group's publication of the pamphlets of the *Tracts for the Times* as "Tractarians," which eventually gave way to "Oxford Movement." Newman and his associates asserted the principle of apostolic succession of bishops, thus asserting the total spiritual independence of the Church of England from the English secular state. This counteracted the current political crisis in the Church of England, but the group's principles went much further than that. Their aim was purely spiritual: to bring about a spiritual reformation of the Church of England. One of the fundamental principles was *antiquity*. They believed that the real Church was made up of three branches, all rooted in the first four centuries of the Christian era: the Roman Catholic Church, the Orthodox Church, and the Anglican Church of England. They insisted that the Anglican Church was a continuation in England of the Roman Catholic Church of the Middle Ages, and hence, there was no severance from its Roman Catholic roots. On the other hand, they advocated that the current Roman Catholic Church, principally due to the teachings of the Council of Trent, erroneously and lacking authority had made additions to the fundamental Catholic doctrines of the early Church. Furthermore, the Tractarians saw themselves as reviving an old tradition in the Anglican Church dating back to the seventeenth century but almost extinguished due to the doctrine promoted by the empirical philosopher and medical doctor John Locke (1632–1704), the "father of liberalism" in matters political and religious,[13] and which was compounded by the ascension of Queen Mary II (1662–1694) and King William III (1650–1702) during the Glorious Revolution in 1688.

The Tractarians insisted that it was anti-Christian to affirm that the secular state had power over the church. This affirmation had a ring of Roman Catholicism and, therefore, the members of the Oxford Movement became known as Anglo-Catholic or High Church Anglicans. They pleaded with the Church of England to revert and reassume its former ways as an undivided church in matters of doctrine, liturgy, and devotion.

Newman wrote the famous *Tract 90* in 1841. It was a courageous essay which clearly indicated that Newman did not rely on the sway of public opinion but was earnestly in search of the truth about the true Church according to his conscience. He was emulating St. Paul, who wrote to the Church in Galatia, "Am I now seeking the favor of men, or of God? Or am I trying to please men? If I were still pleasing men, I should not be a servant of Christ" (Gal. 1:10).

The essay by and large sought to interpret the Anglican Thirty-Nine Articles as being consistent with the Roman Catholic's Council of Trent. Newman's detailed examination of the Thirty-Nine Articles proposed that their framers directed their negations not against Catholicism's authorized creed, but only against popular errors and exaggerations initiated by the Council of Trent. *Tract 90* provoked such substantial criticism and hostile response that no subsequent tract was ever

13 Nancy J. Hirschmann, *Gender, Class, and Freedom in Modern Political Theory* (Princeton University Press, 2009), 79.

published. Matters became compounded when the Oxford Movement faced an inner crisis and a major blow when Newman and others subsequently left the Church of England to become Roman Catholics.[14]

Now, back to Newman as an Anglican priest. The parish of St. Mary provided the benefice of the poor hamlet of Littlemore. As already stated, it was here in 1833 that Newman got caught up with the initial stages of what came to be called the Oxford Movement. The liberalizing activity of the Whig government was the first specifically identified threat to the Church of England.[15] *Liberalism* today has many meanings. What Newman meant by it was doctrinal liberalism, the belief that dogma was an opinion; religion did not possess objective truth, for such a reality did not exist; and one religion was as good as another. Newman immersed himself in a valiant attempt to restore within the Church of England the vitality of the ancient Catholic Church and to keep it from being taken over by liberalism.

The *Tracts for the Times* represented his effort to do so. Newman wrote ten of the twenty tracts that were published by the end of 1833. These tracts emphasized primarily the apostolic succession of bishops and the intrinsic authority of the Church as independent of the secular state. He hoped to secure the cooperation and support of the Evangelicals by writing five letters on church reform in the October and November 1833 issues of the publication *The Record*. He got deeply involved in the successful campaign at Oxford to defeat a bill

[14] "Oxford Movement," in *An Episcopal Dictionary of the Church*, eds. Robert Boak Slocum and Don S. Armentrout (Church Publishing, 2000), online at https://www.episcopalchurch.org/glossary/oxford-movement-the/.

[15] The Whigs, at the time when Newman was still an Anglican priest, were an English political party. Once back in power, the Whigs directly interfered with the activities of the Church of England. For example, they decided which dioceses should be suppressed and which new ones should be created. In other words, they established absolute government control over the church, imposing secular and political agendas.

introduced by the ruling Whig party in Parliament that would have allowed dissenters into the university beginning on August 1, 1834.

However, as already indicated, it was through his homilies that Newman shined and exercised his growing spiritual influence. The first of nine volumes of his homilies was published in 1834. The last volume was published in 1844. He was careful not to attack the personal character of people in writing his opposition to their religious-political beliefs and agendas. He never deviated from this approach throughout his life, first as an Anglican and then as a Roman Catholic.

Newman, by 1836, decided that the faithful at Littlemore should have their own chapel and a school. He managed to raise enough funds to build both structures and dedicated the chapel to St. Mary the Virgin and St. Nicholas. It was here that all his significant activity took place.

Newman became the editor of the *British Critic* in 1836. He provided a series of lectures in a side chapel at Littlemore in defense of his proposed *via media* as an alternative to popular Anglicanism and Roman Catholicism. While his influence became renowned in Oxford around 1839, his study of Monophysitism led him to doubt that Anglican theology was consistent with the principle of ecclesiastical authority, a principle that he came to accept in his journey of discovering the truth regarding the authentic Church.[16] Once he had reached this stage, there was no return.

Another component that led to his doubts was an article by the Anglo-Irish Nicholas Wiseman (later cardinal) entitled "The Anglican Claim," which had been published in the *Dublin Review*. Wiseman quoted St. Augustine's work against the Donatists.[17] Newman would write about his reaction years later in his *Apologia Pro Vita Sua*:

16 Hutton, "Newman," 518.

17 Nicholas Wiseman, "The Anglican Claim," *Dublin Review*, July 1839.

> For a mere sentence, the words of St. Augustine struck me with a power which I never had felt from any words before.... They were like the "Tolle, lege, — Tolle, lege," of the child, which converted St. Augustine himself, "Securus judicat orbis terrarum!" By those great words of the ancient Father, interpreting and summing up the long and varied course of ecclesiastical history, the theology of the Via Media was absolutely pulverized.[18]

Newman continued as a High Anglican controversialist cleric until 1841, when he published *Tract 90*. By then he considered the position of Anglicans to be similar to that of the semi-Arians in the Arian controversy of the early fourth century. The joint Anglican-Lutheran bishopric established in Jerusalem in 1841 by the governments of England and Prussia was to him further evidence that the Church of England had ceased to be apostolic.[19]

Newman withdrew to Littlemore with a small band of followers in 1842. They lived in semi-monastic conditions. He called the building "The House of the Blessed Virgin Mary at Littlemore" (now Newman College).[20] It was here that he began writing his insightful and theologically eminent *An Essay on the Development of Christian Doctrine*.[21] The following year, in February 1843, Newman published his formal retraction of all the harsh things he had previously written against Roman Catholicism and the Pope. He

18 *Apologia Pro Vita Sua*, pt. 5.

19 Hutton, "Newman," 518.

20 Owen Chadwick, *Acton and History* (Cambridge University Press, 2002), 193–194.

21 John Henry Newman, *An Essay on the Development of Christian Doctrine* (London, 1845); I will be citing from the edition presented at The Newman Reader (Longmans, Green and Co., 1909), https://www.newmanreader.org/works/development/index.html#titlepage.

preached his last Anglican sermon at Littlemore, the valedictory "The Parting of Friends," on September 25, 1843, resigned the position at St. Mary's, and withdrew to his own home at Littlemore,[22] living there unnoticed as an Anglican for the next two years; that is, until he was formally received into the Roman Catholic Church.

The major writings which John Henry Newman published as an Anglican minister are *The Arians of the Fourth Century* (1833); *Tracts for the Times* (1833–1841); *British Critic* (1836–1842); *Lyra Apostolica* (poems mostly by Newman and Keble, collected in 1836); *On the Prophetical Office of the Church* (1837); *Lectures on Justification* (1838); *Parochial and Plain Sermons* (1834–1843); *Select Treatises of St. Athanasius* (1842, 1844); *Lives of the English Saints* (1843–44); *Essays on Miracles* (1826, 1843); *Oxford University Sermons* (1843); and *Sermons on Subjects of the Day* (1843).

22 Hutton, "Newman," 518.

TWO

John Henry Newman as Member of the Roman Catholic Church

By 1845, John Henry Newman plainly grasped that his reasoning and arguments regarding the relationship between the Roman Catholic Church and England were stronger than he had previously thought. This exhibits his pristine intellectual honesty, in that he willingly accepted the truth of what he had apprehended on the intellectual level. He saw no alternative but to convert to the Roman Catholic Church. The event took place on October 9, 1845, at the hands of the Italian Passionist priest Blessed Dominic Barberi (1792–1849).[23] Newman had to pay a heavy price for his formal conversion because it produced grave personal consequences: broken relationships with family, friends, and colleagues, as well as the polarization of the attitude toward him in Oxford.[24]

Just as a young Newman felt that he had been called to serve the Lord as an Anglican priest, so, after he became a Catholic, he also discerned a vocation to serve as a Roman Catholic priest. Consequently, he left Oxford in February 1846 and headed for St. Mary's

23 "St. John Henry Newman: Newman's Littlemore Legacy," St. Mary and St. Nicholas Church, http://www.littlemorechurch.org/st-john-henry-newman.html.

24 Gilley, *Newman and His Age*, 243–245.

College, Oscott, where he began his accelerated training for priesthood ordination.

The history of Oscott College is intriguing. It began in the seventeenth century when Roman Catholics still lived under the Penal Laws in England.[25] A local Roman Catholic priest, Fr. Andrew Bromwich (ca. 1640–1702), established a mission in 1694 from his family home, situated in the hamlet locally called *Auscot.* He went about his business under the protection of the 3rd Lord Walter Aston of Forfar (1633–1714), a well-known Roman Catholic. However, this protection evaporated due to the Popish Plot, a fictitious conspiracy invented by the treacherous and excommunicated Catholic priest Titus Oakes (1649–1705) in 1678. He claimed that there was a Catholic conspiracy to murder King Charles II of England. Bromwich survived the harsh measures that resulted from the fabricated conspiracy.

Fr. Bromwich's place was called a "mission." It became a residential school for boys and the training center for Roman Catholic priests. Francis Martyn was the first priest ordained from there in 1805. Oscott College was a flourishing institution by the time John Henry Newman was an Anglican priest. It grew on the heels of the removal of the legal prohibitions for Roman Catholics, enacted in 1829 by the Catholic Emancipation Act. The building soon became cramped, and a new location was sought and established in 1838, and it became the foundation for the revival of Catholicism in Britain.

[25] The penal laws were Parliamentary laws passed against Roman Catholics in Britain and Ireland following the English Reformation. Various acts were passed in the sixteenth and seventeenth centuries that imposed penalties on Catholics, including imprisonment for participating in the Mass, and a prohibition against Catholics voting, holding public office, owning land, teaching, and publishing or selling Catholic literature. These measures were sporadically enforced during the seventeenth century and largely ignored during the eighteenth.

Newman left Oscott and headed for Rome, with his friend Ambrose St. John (1815–1875), in October 1846. The latter had joined Newman at Littlemore. He had already converted to Roman Catholicism from being an Anglican priest about one month before Newman did the same.

The Venerable English College in Rome, named after the Anglo-Saxon theologian, historian, and chronologist Benedictine monk Bede the Venerable (ca. 672–735),[26] was the seminary for English seminarians. However, Newman and St. John opted to study at the Urban College, the Roman seminary that trained priesthood candidates to serve in the missions. By now, Newman was already an established British theologian, academic, philosopher, historian, writer, and poet. He was already a prominent and controversial figure in the religious history of England by the middle of the 1830s.[27] The situation required a huge dosage of humility on the part of Newman and St. John. Most of the other seminarians were about half their age and, obviously, not recognized as great intellectual figures. In any case, Newman frequently visited the Venerable English College and was frequently present at the theological debates that took place there.

Newman was ordained a Roman Catholic priest on June 1, 1847, by Cardinal Giacomo Filippo Fransoni, the Prefect of the Sacred Congregation for the Propagation of the Faith (today's Dicastery for Evangelization). He celebrated his First Mass in that institution at the altar above the shrine of St. Hyacinth on June 5, 1847. Soon thereafter, Pope Blessed Pius IX encouraged the new priest to establish the first Oratory of St. Philip Neri in England. St. John joined him in this undertaking, and both became Oratorians.

[26] Pope Leo XIII canonized him and declared him a Doctor of the Church on November 13, 1899.

[27] Gilley, *Newman and His Age*, 201.

The Confederation of Oratories of St. Philip Neri, commonly known as Oratorians, is a male Catholic society of apostolic life, wherein its members live a common life, bound only by charity, and take no formal vows. It was founded in Rome by St. Philip Neri (1515–1595), deemed to be the second Apostle of Rome. The first community received papal recognition in 1575, soon after the Council of Trent. There are today almost ninety Oratories across the world. Every Oratorian binds himself to a specific, autonomous, self-governing local community. The residence is called an Oratory and usually named after the place it is located.

Newman returned to England toward the end of 1847 as a brand-new Oratorian. He established the first Oratory in England within eight months of his priestly ordination. This Oratory, relocated a number of times, was established first at Maryvale near Birmingham on February 1, 1848 — the year revolutions took place across most of Europe, including the Papal States. It was named Birmingham Oratory. Newman lived there for nearly forty years, except for the four years he was in Ireland.[28]

Many Anglicans felt betrayed when Newman crossed the Tiber and went over to Rome. Like all Catholics of the time in England, but especially for him due to his renowned conversion and subsequent ordination as a Roman Catholic priest, Newman had to deal with rampant anti-Catholicism in his homeland. This deeply rooted, hateful prejudice had formed part of the fabric of English culture since the sixteenth-century English Reformation, initiated by King Henry VIII and aggressively carried on by his son, King Edward VI, and then by his half-sister, Queen Elizabeth I. At the time of Newman, according to D. G. Paz, anti-Catholicism was "an integral part of what it meant to be a Victorian."[29]

[28] Hutton, "Newman," 518.

[29] D. G. Paz, *Popular Anti-Catholicism in Mid-Victorian England* (Stanford University Press, 1992), 299.

This attitude intensified, partly due to Pope Pius IX's papal bull *Universalis Ecclesiae* of September 29, 1850, which reestablished the Roman Catholic hierarchy in England. It had been absent since the death of the last Roman Catholic bishop during the reign of Queen Elizabeth I. The British press, led by *The Times* and *Thackeray's Punch,* lost no time in agitating the Anglican community. They portrayed the reestablishment of the Catholic hierarchy as a papal attempt to reclaim Rome's control over England and dubbed it "papal aggression." Prime Minister John Russell issued a public letter to the Anglican bishop of Durham, Edward Maltby, dated November 7, 1850. He passionately denounced the Pope's decision, portraying it as an attempt to impose a foreign yoke on the minds and consciences of the English people. His aim to stir up a national outcry against the Roman Catholic Church produced a violent reaction. It led to vicious acts across the kingdom against Roman Catholics. Newman, undeterred, rose to the occasion and jumped into the debate. He was keen for Roman Catholic laity to be at the forefront of any public apologetics. Anticipating Vatican Council II (1962–1965) and Pope Francis, he wrote that lay Catholics should "make the excuse of this persecution for getting up a great organization, going round the towns giving lectures, or making speeches."[30] Next, Newman took the initiative and booked the Birmingham Corn Exchange for a series of public lectures. He decided to make their tone popular and provide cheap offprints to those who attended. These became his *Lectures on the Present Position of Catholics in England.* They were delivered weekly, beginning on June 30, and were published on September 1, 1851. He delivered nine lectures: "Protestant View of

30 John Henry Newman, *The Letters and Diaries of John Henry Newman,* vol. 14 (Nelson, 1963), 214.

the Catholic Church"; "Tradition the Sustaining Power of the Protestant View"; "Fable the Basis of the Protestant View"; "True Testimony Insufficient for the Protestant View"; "Logical Inconsistency of the Protestant View"; Prejudice the Life of the Protestant View"; "Assumed Principles of the Intellectual Ground of the Protestant View"; "Ignorance Concerning Catholics the Protection of the Protestant View"; and "Duties of Catholics Towards the Protestant View."[31] Unfortunately, following the first edition, a number of paragraphs were removed as a result of the trial involving the excommunicated and former Italian Catholic priest Giacinto Achilli, wherein a bigoted judge, on June 24, 1852, declared Newman guilty of libel.[32]

In 1862, Newman initiated his preparation for writing autobiographical and other memoranda to defend his ministry as a Roman Catholic priest. It seems that this was initially intended to be a private matter. However, they were published to counteract what was alleged by Charles Kingsley (1819–1875), a stridently anti-Catholic cleric of the Church of England and professor of history at Cambridge University, in his article in *Macmillan's Magazine* in January 1864. The author, in his review of James Anthony Froude's *History of England*, commented that, "Truth for its own sake, had never been a virtue with the Roman clergy. Father Newman informs us that it need not, and on the whole ought not to be." Newman reacted with a robust rebuttal, which he made public.[33] It

[31] John Henry Newman, *Lectures on the Present Position of Catholic in England, Addressed to the Brothers of the Oratory in the Summer of 1851* (Longmans, Green and Co., 1908).

[32] "Achilli v. Newman: Anti-Catholicism in Court," Ecclesiastical History Society, October 18, 2018, https://eccleshistsoc.wordpress.com/2018/10/18/achilli-v-newman-anti-catholicism-in-court/.

[33] Ian Ker, *John Henry Newman: A Biography* (Oxford University Press, 1988), 543.

took the form of a written debate designed for public consumption. Kingsley refrained from admitting any fault. Newman presented his side in a pamphlet entitled *Mr. Kingsley and Dr. Newman: A Correspondence on the Question Whether Dr. Newman Teaches That Truth Is No Virtue.*[34] The writing has been described as "unsurpassed in the English language for the vigor of its satire."[35] Kingsley asserted his defense in a lengthy pamphlet entitled *What Then Does Dr. Newman Mean?*, described by a historian as "one of the most momentous rhetorical and polemical failures of the Victorian age."[36] Newman's response to Kingsley's self-justification was the publication of one of his masterpieces, *Apologia Pro Vita Sua*. It was published in seven installments, beginning on April 21, 1864. An eighth pamphlet was published as an appendix on June 16 of that same year. Newman's *Apologia Pro Vita Sua* narrates the history of his religious views, charting his path from Anglicanism to Roman Catholicism. He sought in part to defend himself from charges of dishonesty; some claimed that he had been secretly Catholic for a long time, outwardly pretending to be Anglican so as to more effectively convert other Anglicans to Catholicism.

The *Apologia Pro Vita Sua* was for the most part warmly received, among Catholics and Anglicans alike. In this way, it was an ecumenical gesture long before the teachings of Vatican II. Newman offered Catholics an accurate description of Protestant views, and Protestants were treated to a closely reasoned defense of Catholic doctrine. As the exchange of ideas continued, Newman polished his arguments. He published a revised version of his work in 1865, and it reached its final form around 1886.

[34] Published in 1864 by Longman, Green, Longman, Roberts and Green.

[35] Hutton, "Newman," 518.

[36] Frank M. Turner, introduction to *Apologia Pro Vita Sua and Six Sermons*, by John Henry Newman (Yale University Press, 2008), 33.

In its original form, the *Apologia Pro Vita Sua* began with two polemical pieces that engaged Charles Kingley directly: "Mr. Kingsley's Method of Disputation" and "True Mode of Meeting Mr. Kingsley."[37] The rest of the book presented a "history of my religious opinions," beginning with Newman's childhood. He presented a detailed account of his religious evolution, including his several conversions, which we have already outlined in chapter 1.

Newman published his *Grammar of Assent* in 1870. His approach was somewhat original in that it was a meticulously reasoned work in which the relevance of religious belief was upheld by arguments, an approach rather different from that commonly used by Catholic theologians at the time. This book was written at a critical point in the history of the Catholic Church: the assembly of Vatican I, its dogmatic definition of Papal Infallibility in matters of faith and morals, and its suspension due to the Italian army's capture of Rome. Newman was apprehensive about the formal definition of this doctrine, which henceforth would bind every Catholic to accept it. He thought the timing was inopportune.[38] However, Newman gave no sign of disapproval when the doctrine was finally defined, but was an advocate of the "principle of minimizing," which included very few papal declarations within the scope of infallibility.[39]

The intellectually honest and faithful Roman Catholic Newman republished his Anglican works in 1877, adding two volumes that contained his defense of the *via media*, a rather long preface in which

[37] These chapters were omitted from subsequent editions. For the context and publication details of the *Apologia*, see Ker, *John Henry Newman*, chap. 14.

[38] John R. Connolly, *John Henry Newman: A View of Catholic Faith for the New Millennium* (Rowman and Littlefield, 2005), 10.

[39] John Henry Newman, *A Letter Addressed to His Grace the Duke of Norfolk* (B.M. Pickering, 1875), 120.

he criticized and counter-argued his very own arguments that were contained in the original works.[40]

Pope Pius IX mistrusted Newman, but this was far from the case with his successor, Pope Leo XIII. Leo was encouraged by Henry Fitzalan-Howard, 15th Duke of Norfolk, and other prominent lay English Catholics to name John Henry Newman a cardinal of the Roman Church. Consequently, during the consistory of May 12, 1879, the Pope created Newman a cardinal, assigning him as cardinal deacon of the Church of San Giorgio al Velabro. Newman's request that he not be ordained a bishop and remain a resident at the Birmingham Oratory was honored.

Newman's health began to fail during the latter part of 1886; he was then eighty-five years old. After being created a cardinal, he returned to the Birmingham Oratory from his last trip to Rome, and resided there for the rest of his life. He celebrated his last Mass on Christmas Day 1889. He died at the Birmingham Oratory on August 11, 1890, as a member of the Birmingham Oratory and a priest and cardinal of the Catholic Church. The cause of his death was pneumonia. He was buried eight days later in the Oratorian cemetery at Rednal Hill, Birmingham. The pall over the coffin bore the motto that Newman adopted for use as a cardinal, *Cor ad cor loquitur* (Heart speaks to heart). On October 2, 2008, workers dug up Newman's grave, so as to relocate the cardinal's remains to Birmingham Oratory to facilitate veneration of the relics by the faithful. They found the grave empty, his coffin and remains apparently completely disintegrated by time and the elements.[41]

[40] Hutton, "Newman," 518–519.

[41] Freddy Gray, "The Venerable John Henry Newman," *Catholic World Report*, May 11, 2011, https://www.catholicworldreport.com/2011/05/11/the-venerable-john-henry-newman/.

Following a thorough investigation and examination of his life, writings, and activities by the Congregation (now Dicastery) for the Causes of Saints, Pope John Paul II proclaimed him Venerable on January 22, 1991. He was declared Blessed by the great Newman admirer Pope Benedict XVI on September 19, 2010, in Birmingham, England. Pope Francis, during the consistory of cardinals on July 1, 2019, announced his intention to canonize Newman, and that Pope entered his name in the annals of the saints on October 13, 2019, during a Mass in St. Peter's Square. By then, there were already many voices calling for St. John Henry Newman to be named a Doctor of the Church.

The major writings which John Henry Newman published as a Roman Catholic are *Essay on the Development of Christian Doctrine* (1845); *Retraction of Anti-Catholic Statements* (1845); *Loss and Gain* (a novel, 1848); *Faith and Prejudice and Other Unpublished Sermons* (1848–1873; collected 1956); *Discourses to Mixed Congregations* (1849); *Difficulties of Anglicans* (1850); *The Present Position of Catholics in England* (1851); *The Idea of a University* (1852 and 1858); *Cathedra Sempiterna* (1852); *Callista* (a novel,1855); *On Consulting the Faithful in Matters of Christian Doctrine* (1859); *The Rambler* (two editorials, 1859–1860); *Apologia Pro Vita Sua* (religious autobiography, 1864; revised edition, 1865; final revision, ca. 1886); *Letter to Dr. Pusey* (1865); and *The Dream of Gerontius* (1865).

THREE

Popes and Cardinal John Henry Newman

Postulatory letters are formal requests submitted to a higher authority. In the case of Cardinal St. John Henry Newman, these letters were submitted directly to Pope Francis and specifically asked him to declare the saint a Doctor of the Roman Catholic Church. The list of these letters is long and very impressive. They come from every corner of the world and are not restricted to Catholic petitioners. There are requests from many conferences of Catholic bishops, Anglican archbishops and bishops, Catholic and non-Catholic universities and other academic institutions, Catholic and non-Catholic scholars, as well as prominent prelates. Even the University of Oxford, where Newman studied, and Oriel College, where Newman not only taught but also suffered much personal pain of rejection and misunderstanding, make the list. What is of great interest is that all the aforementioned inherently recognize that only the Roman Catholic Pontiff has the exclusive competence and authority to make such a decision and declaration. Another fact is that Newman's writings are considered to belong to the sphere of ecumenism.

We might ask why such an extraordinary request has been made by shepherds within the Catholic Church, joined with other religious and academic leaders, both Catholic and non-Catholic. The answer is rather simple: Cardinal John Henry

Newman enjoys an extraordinary, worldwide importance and appeal because his eminent teachings are deemed to be highly relevant to our own times.

Cardinal Newman is considered as one of the forerunners of Vatican II, as well as one of the spiritual writers who has greatly influenced both Catholic and other Christian theologies since the nineteenth century. He presented a thinking that was classical, with a deep respect for tradition, while also opening new avenues within Catholic theology and spirituality that have proven to be most prophetic and fruitful with the passage of time. Though Pope Pius IX was suspicious of the saint's writings, the public vindication of Newman's writings was rendered by Pope Leo XIII when he created Newman a cardinal. Leo's papal successors down to our own time also spoke about the profound theological wisdom of the saint.

Newman became a Catholic priest during the last year of the papacy of Gregory XVI (reigned 1831–1846) and continued to serve under the pontificates of Pius IX and Leo XIII. As already indicated elsewhere, Pope Pius IX, skeptical of novel ideas, was suspicious of the teachings of Newman, though of course he never even whispered a word of condemnation. Pope Leo XIII succeeded Pius IX in 1878. He was immensely impressed by Newman's deep theological insights and teachings. He, like Newman, had also been an object of attacks in the media when he was the Archbishop of Perugia, Italy (1846–1880). As already indicated, this Pope consented to the request submitted to name Newman a cardinal. This took place a year after the intellectual, forward-thinking, diplomatic, and witty Cardinal Gioacchino Vincenzo Pecci had been elected Pope on February 20, 1878. He would be fondly called the "Pope of the workers" and the "Rosary Pope."

In the years since Newman's death, succeeding Popes have spoken about him on numerous occasions. The most prolific was Pope Benedict XVI. Perhaps there was a deep affinity between the saint and this Pope. When Benedict made the courageous decision to resign the papacy, he was doing what Newman had done in becoming a Catholic. Pope Benedict XVI followed his conscience when he announced his papal abdication on February 11, 2013,[42] notwithstanding the longstanding tradition that Popes die in office and, moreover, putting aside what Catholics and non-Catholics alike would say about his historic decision. The supremacy of conscience was just as compelling to Pope Benedict XVI as it had been to Cardinal Newman.

The following is the official notice of March 15, 1879, of Pope Leo XIII's intention to create the Oratorian Fr. John Henry Newman as a cardinal:

> The Holy Father deeply appreciating the genius and learning which distinguish you, your piety, the zeal displayed by you in the exercise of the Holy Ministry, your devotion and filial attachment to the Holy Apostolic See, and the signal services you have for long years rendered to religion, has decided on giving you a public and solemn proof of his esteem and good-will. And to this end he will deign to raise you to the honors of the Sacred Purple, in the next Consistory, the precise day of which will be notified to you in due time.
>
> In forwarding you this joyful announcement by its fitting and prescribed channel, I cannot refrain from congratulating your Paternity on seeing your merits rewarded

[42] Pope Benedict XVI's resignation took effect on February 28, 2013.

in so splendid a manner by the august Head of the Church, and I rejoice in heart that I shall very soon have you as a colleague in the Sacred Senate, of which you will not fail to be one of the chief ornaments.

Accept, I entreat you, this expression of my regard, and at the same time the assurance of the particular esteem with which I sign myself.[43]

Pope Pius X

Cardinal Giuseppe Melchiorre Sarto was born in Riese, Kingdom of Lombardy–Venetia, then part of the Austrian Empire (now in the province of Treviso, Veneto, Italy), on June 2, 1835. He was the second of ten children. The family was poor, but his parents valued education. Giuseppe, nicknamed "Bepi" by his mother, walked almost four miles each day to school. He was an exuberant boy by nature, and his teacher frequently disciplined him. Yet he was an excellent student, who prayed on his own for ten minutes every day at church before returning home from school. He often carried his shoes to make them last longer. His schoolmates often teased him for his shabby clothes and meager lunches. When he was eleven years old, he had told his father that he wanted to become a priest. Once in the seminary, he shined as a student and finished his classical, philosophical, and theological studies with distinction. He was ordained a priest on September 18, 1858. Afterward he continued studying more deeply on his own the subjects of theology and canon law, while carrying on his priestly duties. Pope Leo XIII appointed him bishop of Mantua on November 10, 1884. The same Pope created him a cardinal and named him Patriarch of Venice on June 12, 1893. He was

[43] Quoted in Wilfrid Ward, *The Life of John Henry Cardinal Newman Based on His Private Journals and Correspondence*, vol. 2 (Longmans, Green and Co., 1912), 582–583.

elected Pope on August 4, 1903, during a tempestuous conclave — the last one in which secular powers interfered in a papal election by lodging a "papal veto" against one of the cardinals.

Cardinal Sarto chose the name Pius X (1903–1914). As Pope, among many things, he improved priestly formation, introduced liturgical reforms, and began the reform and the first ever codification of canon law for the Latin side of the Church. He was the one who allowed children to make their First Holy Communion when they reached the age of reason, around age seven. He was preoccupied with modernist ideas, which began to infiltrate the Catholic Church and which he eventually officially condemned as heretical in his encyclical *Pascendi Dominici Gregis* of July 3, 1907. Furthermore, he bound every member of the Roman Catholic clergy to take an oath against Modernism. He died of a broken heart with the imminent onset of World War I (1914–1918). His body was exhumed on May 19, 1944, for inspection. This was part of the Beatification process for his cause to be eventually declared a Saint. His unembalmed body was found miraculously incorrupt. He now rests underneath the Altar of the Visitation in St. Peter's Basilica. Pope Pius XII declared him Blessed on June 3, 1951, and subsequently a Saint on May 29, 1954.

Cardinal John Henry Newman was already dead for about eighteen years when Pope Pius X wrote the following letter to Bishop Edward Thomas O'Dwyer of Limerick, Ireland, on March 10, 1908, praising Newman for his profound and insightful writings. The letter stated:

> Venerable Brother, greetings and Our Apostolic blessing. We hereby inform you that your essay, in which you show that the writings of Cardinal Newman, far from being in disagreement with Our Encyclical Letter *Pascendi*, are very much in harmony with it, has been emphatically approved by Us: for you could not have better served both the truth and the dignity of

man.... And indeed, in the domain of England, it is common knowledge that John Henry Newman pleaded the cause of the Catholic faith in his prolific literary output so effectively that his work was both highly beneficial to its citizens and greatly appreciated by Our Predecessors: and so he is held worthy of office whom Leo XIII, undoubtedly a shrewd judge of men and affairs, appointed Cardinal; indeed he was very highly regarded by him at every stage of his career, and deservedly so. Truly, there is something about such a large quantity of work and his long hours of labor lasting far into the night that seems foreign to the usual way of theologians; nothing can be found to bring any suspicion about his faith. You correctly state that it is entirely to be expected that while no new signs of heresy were apparent, he has perhaps used an off-guard manner of speaking to some people in certain places, but that what the Modernists do is to falsely and deceitfully take those words out of the whole context of what he meant to say and twist them to suit their own meaning. We therefore congratulate you for having, through your knowledge of all his writings, brilliantly vindicated the memory of this eminently upright and wise man from injustice: and also for having, to the best of your ability, brought your influence to bear among your fellow-countrymen, but particularly among the English speaking people, so that those who were accustomed to abusing his name and deceiving the ignorant should henceforth cease doing so. Would that they should follow Newman the author faithfully by studying his books without, to be sure, being addicted to their own prejudices, and let them not with wicked cunning conjure anything up from them or declare that their own opinions are confirmed in them; but instead let them understand his pure and whole

> principles, his lessons and inspiration which they contain. They will learn many excellent things from such a great teacher: in the first place, to regard the Magisterium of the Church as sacred, to defend the doctrine handed down inviolately by the Fathers and, what is of highest importance to the safeguarding of Catholic truth, to follow and obey the Successor of St. Peter with the greatest faith.[44]

Pope Pius XI

Cardinal Ambrogio Damiano Achille Ratti of Milan was elected as Pope Pius XI (1922–1939) on February 6, 1922, on the fourteenth ballot of the longest conclave of the twentieth century. He was a great intellectual, a great administrator, a polyglot, athletic, and most courageous in standing up to Benito Mussolini and Adolf Hitler. The autonomous country of the Vatican City State was established on February 11, 1929, during his papacy. He wrote an encyclical entitled *Ad Salutem Humani* on April 20, 1930, to commemorate the fifteenth centenary of the death of St. Augustine. Part of the encyclical speaks about the Donatist heresy, which Newman wrote about as an Anglican priest and which he feared the Church of England was duplicating and perhaps had succumbed to.[45] The Pope referred to Newman's *Apologia Pro Vita Sua* without specifically naming him when he wrote the following:

> When our Saint [Augustine], therefore, in refutation of the Donatists who dared to confine the true Church of Christ within the narrow bounds of a corner of Africa, maintained

[44] Pius X, "*Epistola Qua Pius PP. X approbat opusculum Episcopi Limericiensis circa scripta Card. Newman,*" *Acta Sanctae Sedis,* vol. 41, 1908; trans. Michael Davies, Newman Reader, https://newmanreader.org/canonization/popes/acta10mar08.html.

[45] *Apologia Pro Vita Sua,* 116–117.

> the universality or "catholicity" of a Church in which all men may find the help and protection of the aids of Divine grace, he rightly closed his reasoning with these solemn words: "The decision is sure in which the world concurs." The reading of this phrase, not so very long ago, influenced to such a degree a man of high fame and noble nature, that he did not tarry long in entering the one Fold of Christ.[46]

Pope Pius XII

Cardinal Eugenio Pacelli was the former secretary of state[47] under Pope Pius XI when he was elected as Pope Pius XII (1939–1958) on March 2, 1939. He celebrated his sixty-sixth birthday on that day. It was just before the outbreak of World War II. He was the first secretary of state to be elected Pope since Clement IX (1667–1669). Pacelli came from Roman nobility, had vast diplomatic experience, was a linguist, and as Pope was dead set against communism. He was the Pope who began reversing the longstanding dominance of Italians in the College of Cardinals by appointing more non-Italians than any Pope before him, beginning a gradual internationalization of the Vatican. He had a soft spot for Americans, and he elevated several American prelates to the cardinalate[48] and named many Americans to powerful Church posts.[49] He praised Cardinal Newman for his enduring search

[46] Pius XI, *Ad Salutem* (April 20, 1930), no. 15, https://www.papalencyclicals.net/pius11/p11salut.htm.

[47] All cardinals in the Roman Curia, except those belonging to the three apostolic tribunals (Signatura, Roman Rota, Penitentiary), cease in their curial office when a Pope dies or abdicates. It is totally up to the new Pope to either reappoint or dismiss them.

[48] For example, Cardinals Francis Spellman of New York and James McIntyre of Los Angeles.

[49] For example, Archbishops Joseph P. Hurley, Gerald P. O'Hara, and Aloisius Joseph Muench. The last was created a cardinal by Pope John XXIII.

of truth in a letter to Archbishop Bernard Griffin of Westminster, England. The letter was written on April 12, 1945, ten months before Griffin was named a cardinal. Pius XII wrote:

> A century has now all but run its course since John Henry Newman, the pride of Britain and of the universal Church, came to harbor after his long voyage in search of Catholic truth. With anxious and loving care he had sought it; with ready assent he acknowledged at last the warning accents of the Divine Voice. You, as the president of the English and Welsh Hierarchies, have written to Us most dutifully, in your own name and that of your fellow Bishops, with the request that We should share with you this happy opportunity for recalling his memory. Such a request must not go unheeded; We bear you a father's love, and you have good cause for rejoicing....
>
> One quality especially seems to Us to call for close attention and study in the career of the great man whose happy return to the Christian fold you are commemorating. He "gave up his whole life to the truth"; all his efforts, all his untiring labors, were dedicated to that end. A time came when the beauty of Catholic teaching revealed itself clearly to his longing eyes; with that, no obstacle of any kind — his old prejudices, loss of prospects, the protests of his friends — could hold him back; nothing must stand between him and full adherence to the truth he had now mastered. He held to it ever afterwards with unshaken consistency, made it the guiding principle of his whole life, found in it, as in nothing else, full contentment of mind.
>
> Beyond question, revered Brother, among the many important gifts which will make a later posterity honor the

greatness of John Henry Newman, this is his chief title to fame. "The mind," we are told, "knows no food more appetizing than discovery of the truth." What shall we say, then, of truth in matters of religious belief, so intimately bound up with every man's hope of eternal salvation? To search out such truth as this with all care, hunt it down with all eagerness, is a task for great and generous hearts; to possess it fully, is to win enlargement and satisfaction of mind. There can be no doubt that the evocation of so great a memory will have great value for those who already rest in the bosom of the Catholic Church, already enjoy Christian teaching in its entirety. But We think it will be equally valuable to those persons, not rare in your own country, who are in search of the uncontaminated tradition of heavenly truth. They are urged on by this stimulus today more strongly than ever; they look to the See founded by the Prince of the Apostles, to the Mother-city of Rome, with eyes unclouded by prejudice; they have learned to reverence, here, the hallowed cradle of the Christian religion. Towards all these Our heart goes out in fervent love; what heavenly joys of consolations can We best ask for them, foresee for them? The same, surely, in which John Henry Newman, resting now from all those troubles, cares and anxieties, found at last, even in this earthly exile, happiness, and refreshment, and content.[50]

Pope John XXIII

Cardinal Angelo Giuseppe Roncalli was Patriarch of Venice when he was elected Pope on October 28, 1958. He took the name of John XXIII

50 Pope Pius XII, "The Service of Truth," Letter to the Archbishop of Westminster for the Newman Centenary, published in *The Tablet*, October 13, 1945, Newman Reader, https://www.newmanreader.org/canonization/popes/tablet13oct45.html.

(reigned 1958–1963).[51] His election, which was a great surprise, took place on the eleventh ballot. Due to his age of seventy-six, he was expected to be a "caretaker" Pope after the nineteen-year pontificate of Pius XII. His election was only the first surprise. The second surprise came when, on January 25, 1959, he called the Second Ecumenical Council of the Vatican. He was a seasoned diplomat and a solid Church historian, who helped the Jewish underground in saving thousands of refugees in Europe, especially when the Nazis came to power in Germany. His affable personality earned him the nickname "the Good Pope." His short pontificate made a major impact on the Catholic Church, opening her up to dramatic, unexpected changes that were promulgated at Vatican II and occurred through his own dealings with other Christian churches through ecumenism and his relationship with nations. The objective was to open the Church to contemporary culture without losing her unalterable mission and teachings. Thus, he emphasized the Church's pastoral role and her necessary involvement in world affairs. He was the first Pope to name cardinals from Africa, the Philippines, and Japan. He was declared Blessed by Pope John Paul II on September 3, 2000, and canonized by Pope Francis on April 27, 2014. Both ceremonies took place in St. Peter's Square.

Pope John XXIII issued his first encyclical, entitled *Ad Petri Cathedram,* on June 29, 1959, in which he made a distinct reference to Cardinal Newman. It appears in paragraph 71:

> The Catholic Church, of course, leaves many questions open to the discussion of theologians. She does this to the extent

[51] There was a previous papal claimant, Baldassarre Cossa, who carried the name of John XXIII (1410–1415). He was invalidly elected during the Western Schism (1378–1417), in opposition to the legitimate Pope Gregory XII (1406–1415), who resigned the papacy on July 4, 1415. The Council of Constance (1414–1418) deposed the anti-pope John XXIII on May 25, 1415. He submitted to Pope Martin V (1417–1431) a few days before he died on December 22, 1419.

> that matters are not absolutely certain. Far from jeopardizing the Church's unity, controversies, as a noted English author, John Henry Cardinal Newman, has remarked, can actually pave the way for its attainment. For discussion can lead to fuller and deeper understanding of religious truths; when one idea strikes against another, there may be sparks (cf. J. H. Newman, Difficulties of Anglicans, v. 1, 261 ff.).[52]

Pope Paul VI

Cardinal Giovanni Battista Montini was the Archbishop of Milan, Italy, when he was elected as Pope Paul VI (1963–1978) on June 21, 1963. He had been deemed eligible to the papacy for the 1958 conclave which elected Pope John XXIII, but was not yet a cardinal. As it turned out, he was elected Pope John XXIII's immediate successor.

Pope Paul VI was a seasoned diplomat, beginning his career in the Roman Curia at age twenty-five in 1922, two years after his priesthood ordination. He worked very closely for many years with Pope Pius XII as a member of the Vatican Secretariat of State. The Pope revealed that Montini had declined the cardinal's hat. He became Archbishop of Milan in 1954. During his tenure there, he exhibited a genuine ecumenical spirit, adopted new approaches to reach the faithful through pastoral care, embarked on building one hundred new churches, and was considered a liberal prelate. He was created a cardinal by his friend, the newly elected Pope John XXIII, on December 15, 1958.

When a Pope dies while an Ecumenical Council is in session, the Council is automatically suspended and the new Pope has total liberty to either continue or stop it. Pope Paul VI decided to continue

[52] John XXIII, Encyclical Letter on Truth, Unity and Peace *Ad Petri Cathedram* (June 29, 1959). Unless otherwise indicated, all citations of papal and other Vatican documents are taken from the Vatican website, www.vatican.va.

Vatican II, which he closed on December 8, 1965. He ushered in numerous inner Church reforms, despite the conflicting interpretations and controversies attached to the Council. Among many things, he established the Synod of Bishops as a permanent institution on September 14, 1965, put into effect the reform of the Roman Curia, asked all bishops to submit their resignation to the Roman Pontiff when they reached age seventy-five, increased the membership of the College of Cardinals to 120 and denied the papal electoral vote to cardinals upon reaching age eighty, reformed the Liturgy (which would cause great controversies and even the Lefebvre schism), energetically promoted ecumenism, and engaged with the world and secular states through diplomacy.

Pope Paul VI began a process that is still in effect today. He was nicknamed "the Pilgrim Pope" in light of his frequent international pastoral travels. His pontificate witnessed many historic meetings and agreements. He was the first Pope in Church history to make a pilgrimage to Israel, in 1964.

Pope Francis declared him Blessed on October 19, 2014, and a Saint on October 14, 2018. Both ceremonies took place in St. Peter's Square.

Pope Paul VI had a deep admiration of Cardinal Newman. He wrote and spoke about him on a number of occasions. The first one was during his homily on the occasion of the Beatification of Blessed Dominic Barbieri, a Passionist missionary priest, on October 27, 1963, which was a few months after he was elected Pope. As already indicated, Blessed Dominic had received Newman into the Roman Catholic Church. Pope Paul stated:

> "He had a great love for England." Thus did Newman write of this new Beatus, Father Dominic of the Mother of God.

> This phrase would seem to define the figure of this humble but great follower of the Gospel of Christ....
>
> "He had a great love for England." Newman's phrase, if properly meditated upon, means that the love of the pious Religious, the Roman missionary, was directed to Newman himself, the promoter and representative of the Oxford Movement, which raised so many religious questions, and excited such great spiritual energies; to him who, in full consciousness of his mission — "I have a work to do" — and guided solely by love of the truth and fidelity to Christ, traced an itinerary, the most toilsome, but also the greatest, the most meaningful, the most conclusive, that human thought ever travelled during the last century, indeed one might say during the modern era, to arrive at the fullness of wisdom and of peace.
>
> And if that phrase was true and salutary for so distinguished a representative of a great people, so high an authority of a time like ours, will it not be still true and salutary today, in heaven, in the heart of this beloved Beatus, and here below, in the hearts of all those who celebrate his glory, and wish to imitate his example?[53]

Pope Paul VI wrote a message to Bishop Lèon Lommel of Luxembourg on the occasion of the Newman Congress entitled "The Wealth of Cardinal Newman's Thought" and dated May 17, 1970. He wrote about Cardinal Newman, comparing him to the great theologian St. Augustine:

[53] Paul VI, *Discorso di Paolo VI ai Pellegrini Convenuti per la Beatificazione di Domenico della Madre di Dio* (Homily for the Beatification of Bl. Dominic of the Mother of God), October 27, 1963.

The profound change that disturbs the world and the Church and whose effects we experience more and more every day make our contact with Newman's thought ever more precious. His thinking was deeply grounded in the faith and, at the same time, was in close harmony with the best of the demands of intelligence and modern feelings. Like St. Augustine, Newman knew what it cost in suffering to discover the full truth. He recalls to our mind that the search for the truth is an irresistible need of the human spirit and that "to discover the truth, it is indispensable to seek it with a great seriousness of purpose" (*Sermons Universitaires,* I, 8; trad. P. Renaudin, in *Textes Newmaniens,* t. I, Paris, Desclée de Brouwer, 1955, 62). Confident in the intelligence of man and in the action of grace which penetrates it from within, Newman invites us to deepen our understanding of the faith with serenity, and to foster the development of conscience strengthened by the Holy Spirit, in fidelity to the Gospel, after the example of the Virgin Mary (See ibid., XV, 3, 328).

Newman also teaches us to discern the invisible through the visible, for "what we see is but the outward shell of an eternal kingdom; and on that kingdom we fix the eyes of our faith (*Parochial and Plain Sermons* IV, 13; trad. A. Roucou-Barthélémy, in *Pensées sur l'Eglise,* Paris, Cerf, *Unam Sanctam* 30, 1956, 20). Rooted in the heart of the mystery of existence variable as the sky, changeable as the wind, turbulent as the ocean, the penetrating meditation of Newman leads him little by little — one step is enough for me — to the Kindly Light whose brightness clears up misunderstandings and doubts, and whose certitude is the source of serenity for the mind and peace for the heart. It is good for us to hear this great voice denounce the harm of a morbid and conceited criticism, and remind us that everyone "can be fooled by appearances or false reasonings, influenced by prejudices, led astray by too vivid an imagination" and that we must "remain humble because we are ignorant, prudent because we realize our weakness, docile because we truly desire to learn (*University Sermons*, I, 13, trad. Renaudin, op. cit., 66–67), in a free and reasoned attachment to the magisterium of the Church: "The Church is the mother of the great and the small, of those who govern and those who obey. *Securus judicat orbis terrarum*" (Letter to Father Loyson, Nov. 24, 1870 in *Pensées sur l'Eglise*, op. cit., 117).

Newman's profound attachment to the Church is on a par with a demanding respect for the incomparable dignity of the human person, for the unique and irreplaceable character of the person's vocation and his immediate responsibilities before God. He glorifies conscience: "which he does not hesitate to define as the aboriginal vicar of Christ; a prophet in its informations, a monarch in its peremptoriness, a priest in its blessings and anathemas" (*Certain Difficulties felt by Anglicans in Catholic Teaching*, II, 2; trad. in *Pensées sur l'Eglise*, op. cit., 130). But Newman immediately explains what he means by "conscience as I have just described it, and not this miserable pretense which today assumes the name of conscience. The Christian must conquer this base, narrow and proud spirit of his nature which prompts him, as soon as he hears of a forthcoming order, to oppose the superior who gave this order, to question whether or not he exceeds his rights, to rejoice in introducing skepticism in moral and practical questions" (ibid., 131). This remark is of amazing timeliness, like so many insights which have by no means exhausted their fruitfulness for the Church.

Today when everything is being systematically questioned, we can undoubtedly derive much profit by becoming imbued with the profound views of the "Essay on the Development of the Christian Doctrine" (See, for example, Jean Guitton, *La Philosophie de Newman*, Paris, Boivin, 1933) on the organic development of the Church's doctrine, linked to the growth of her living body through the vicissitudes of twenty centuries of history, where truths not yet formulated and latent convictions gradually take on a definite expression under the influence of the Spirit. Nor can we fail to notice the value of the analyses in the "Grammar of Assent" for the modern man who, influenced by new philosophical trends, can hardly find the way to a verifiable certitude, that is, one not linked to a fleeting and changing sincerity, but rooted in a reasoned conviction which may well lean on interior experience, but rests first of all on an objective revelation.

Such is the fruitful timeliness of Newman, after a Council that specified the permanent identity of the Church through the passage of time, while giving renewed expression to the mystery of its profound life and its answer to modern man's inquiries. In this way, it gives testimony to its prodigious power of renewal and its eternal youth. Like Newman, may we discover that "God may be teaching us and offering us knowledge of His ways, if we will but open our eyes, in all the ordinary matters of the day" (*Parochial and Plain Sermons* IV, 249). With Newman, may we advance in the Church with the same love for the truth, the same keen sense of God, the same prudent spiritual discernment, the same familiar piety of the invisible world, the same profound taste for the spiritual, *ex*

> *umbris et imaginibus in veritatem*. Finally, with Newman, "Let us pray to God to give us the beauty of holiness, which consists in tender and eager affection towards our Lord and Savior: which is, in the case of Christians, what beauty of person is to the outward man, so that through God's mercy our souls may have, not strength of health only but a sort of bloom and comeliness; and that as we grow older in body, we may, year by year, grow more youthful in spirit" (*Parochial Sermons* VII, X, 134; trad. in *Méditations et priéres,* M.A. Pératé, Paris, Gabalda, 1916, XXX).[54]

The sainted Pope presented Newman as a prophet when he spoke about him to the participants in the Cardinal Newman Academic Symposium on April 7, 1975. He clearly linked Newman's writings to their application to the religious problems being faced by the Church in the third quarter of the twentieth century, and also stressed Newman's farsighted contribution to ecumenism. Furthermore, he indicated Newman's contribution to Vatican II, which took place in the century following his death. The Pope was crystal clear that Newman's writings were an unquestionable source of enlightenment to the life of the Church after his death.[55] He stated:

> It is with special joy that we have acceded to your wish to be received by us in audience during the Cardinal Newman Academic Symposium now taking place here in Rome and of

[54] Paul VI, "The Wealth of Cardinal Newman's Thought" (address to Newman Congress, May 17, 1970), published in *L'Osservatore Romano* (English edition), June 4, 1970, 114; Newman Reader, https://www.newmanreader.org/canonization/popes/or4jun70.html.

[55] Wilfrid Ward, *The Life of John Henry Cardinal Newman* (Longmans, Green and Co., 1912), 202.

which you are the expert participants.... As students of the great Cardinal, you have come together to deepen your knowledge of Newman's life and thought, and to draw from his powerful example and teachings practical conclusions and responses to the many religious problems of the present day. The echo that your worthy initiative has had among the many admirers of Cardinal Newman throughout the world and the presence among you of many young people are unmistakable signs of the great attraction to Newman and of the relevance that he enjoys today—indeed today perhaps more than at any previous time. We offer a warm greeting to those among you who are members of the Anglican clergy and who by your participation in the Symposium emphasize the great ecumenical importance of the figure and work of Newman at the present time.

He who was convinced of being faithful throughout his life, with all his heart devoted to the light of truth, today becomes an ever brighter beacon for all who are seeking an informed orientation and sure guidance amid the uncertainties of the modern world—a world which he himself prophetically foresaw. Many of the problems which he treated with wisdom—although he himself was frequently misunderstood and misinterpreted in his own time—were the subjects of the discussion and study of the Fathers of the Second Vatican Council, as for example the question of ecumenism, the relationship between Christianity and the world, the emphasis on the role of the laity in the Church and the relationship of the Church to non-Christian religions. Not only this Council but also the present time can be considered in a special way as Newman's hour, in which, with confidence in divine providence, he placed his great hopes and expectations: "Perhaps my name is to be turned to account as a sanction and outset by which others who agree with me in opinion should write and publish instead of me, and thus begin the transmission of views in religious and intellectual matters congenial with my own, to the generation after me" (Cf. W. Ward, *The Life of John Henry Cardinal Newman*, London 1912, vol. 2, 202). And it is precisely the present moment that suggests, in a particularly pressing and persuasive way, the study and diffusion of Newman's thought.

This is not the time for a detailed description of the wide program that the needs of the present moment place before you, the expert scholars and friends of Newman. The very theme of your Symposium, "Newman's Realization of Christian Life," is related to the central purpose of the Council and of the Holy Year.

The "realization" of the Christian ideal in Newman's sense is but another name for a continual effort for the renewal of personal and community life in the spirit of the Gospel and in accordance with the just demands of the present moment of history. "Realizing" our Christian vocation means, in Newman's view, making the truths of our faith a living reality, full of practical consequences for daily life; it means becoming true followers of Christ. And, in the lofty and arduous task to which this Holy Year urgently calls us, the thought and example of John Henry Newman bring a precious light and a great incitement. May his prayer become ours too: "Enable me to believe as if I saw; let me have Thee always before me as if Thou wert always bodily and sensibly present. Let me ever hold

> communion with Thee, my hidden, but my living God" (*Meditations and Devotions*).
>
> It is our hope that your Symposium on Newman's life and thought will bear abundant fruit and offer its own specific and valuable contribution to the Holy Year, for a profound renewal in the life of the Church. We accompany your work with our prayers, invoking upon you all light and strength from the Lord.[56]

Pope Paul VI, in his last address to a group of Bishops from England on their *ad limina* visit on November 10, 1977,[57] spoke about Newman's fidelity to the teachings of the Roman Catholic Church. It would be the last time this Pope spoke about Newman. He told the English bishops:

> Your own Cardinal Newman understood so well the demands of this fidelity, and how the organic development of Christian doctrine must be in complete harmony with pure apostolic faith. And many other countrymen of yours have stressed in their writings the dynamic character and beneficent effects of the Catholic faith.[58]

Pope John Paul II

Cardinal Karol Józef Wojtyła was elected Pope on October 22, 1978. He took the name John Paul II (1978–2005). He hailed from Poland and was the first non-Italian Pope since the Dutchman Adrian VI (1522–1523) had been elected Pope 455 years before. He was a great

[56] Paul VI, "Address to the Participants in the Cardinal Newman Academic Symposium," April 7, 1974.

[57] Pope Paul VI died the following August 6, 1978.

[58] Paul VI, "Address to a Group of Bishops from England on their 'Ad Limina' Visit," November 10, 1977.

intellectual, a polyglot, greatly beloved across the world, and immensely popular within and outside the Catholic Church. He was one of the most traveled world leaders in history, visiting 129 countries during his pontificate. He fought against dictatorships while promoting democracy, and he played a vital role in ending Communist rule in his native Poland and the rest of Eastern Europe.[59] Under John Paul II, the Catholic Church greatly extended her influence in Africa and Latin America, while keeping her influence in Europe and the rest of the world. He established the World Youth Days in 1985 and presided over nine of them. John Paul II was proclaimed Venerable by his close friend and successor, Benedict XVI, on December 19, 2009, and Blessed on May 1, 2011. Pope Francis declared him a Saint, along with Pope John XXIII, on April 27, 2014.

Pope John Paul II was not yet Pope six months when, on April 7, 1979, he wrote a letter to Archbishop George Dwyer of Birmingham, England, to mark the centenary of when John Henry Newman was created a cardinal in 1879. He portrayed Cardinal Newman as one of the great witnesses to the Roman Catholic Faith, with far-reaching implications because of his brilliant writings, with their ecumenical tone, writings which proved to be prophetic. The Pope also spoke about Newman's contribution to Vatican II. He encouraged people to study Newman's profound writings. He wrote:

> In spiritual communion and with pastoral solicitude I gladly respond to your invitation to celebrate together with the Church throughout England the centenary of the elevation to the Cardinalate of one of her great sons and witnesses of the faith, John Henry Newman, created Cardinal of the Holy

59 John Lenczowski, "Public Diplomacy and the Lessons of the Soviet Collapse: The Record and Its Implications," *Journal of Cold War Studies* 6, no. 1 (Winter 2004): 75–89.

Roman Church by my venerable predecessor Leo XIII on 12 May 1879, with the title of Saint George in Velabro.

The elevation of Newman to the Cardinalate, like his conversion to the Catholic Church, is an event that transcends the simple historical fact, as well as the importance it had for his own country. The two events have long since been deeply inscribed in ecclesial life far beyond the shores of England. The providential meaning and importance of these events for the Church at large have been seen more clearly in the course of our own century. Newman himself, with almost prophetic vision, was convinced that he was working and suffering for the defense and affirmation of the cause of religion and of the Church not only in his own time but also in the future. His inspiring influence as a great teacher of the faith and as a spiritual guide is being ever more clearly perceived in our own day, as was pointed out by Paul VI in his address to the Cardinal Newman Academic Symposium during the Holy Year 1975: He (Newman) who was convinced of being faithful throughout his life, with all his heart devoted to the light of truth today becomes an ever brighter beacon for all who are seeking an informed orientation and sure guidance amid the uncertainties of the modern world — a world which he himself prophetically foresaw.

In raising John Henry Newman to the Cardinalate, Leo XIII wished to defend and honor his activity and mission in the Church. Acceding to the earnest desire expressed by members of the English laity under the leadership of the Duke of Norfolk, the Pope meant to pay tribute to the genius of Newman and to give public expression to his own personal appreciation of Newman's merits. He intended to recognize the value of Newman's many writings in defense of God and the Church. In this way Pope Leo upheld and encouraged all those—inside and outside the Catholic Church—who regarded Newman as their spiritual teacher and guide in the way of holiness. Newman himself made this comment on the Pope's intentions: He judged it would give pleasure to English Catholics, and even to Protestant England, if I received some mark of his favor.

The philosophical and theological thought and the spirituality of Cardinal Newman, so deeply rooted in and enriched by Sacred Scripture and the teachings of the Fathers, still retain their particular originality and value. As a leading figure of the Oxford Movement, and later as a promoter of authentic renewal in the Catholic Church, Newman is seen to have a special ecumenical vocation not only for his own country but also for the whole Church. By insisting that the Church must be prepared for converts, as well as converts prepared for the Church, he already in a certain measure anticipated in his broad theological vision one of the main aims and orientations of the Second Vatican Council and the Church in the post-conciliar period. In the spirit of my predecessors in the See of Peter, I express the hope that under this very important aspect, and under other aspects no less important, the figure and teaching of the great Cardinal will continue to inspire an ever more effective fulfilment of the Church's mission in the modern world, and that it will help to renew the spiritual life of her members and hasten the restoration of unity among all Christians.

It is my hope that this centenary will be for all of us an opportunity for studying more closely the inspiring thought of Newman's genius, which speaks to us of deep intellectual honesty, fidelity to conscience and grace, piety and priestly

> zeal, devotion to Christ's Church and love of her doctrine, unconditional trust in divine providence and absolute obedience to the will of God.
>
> I also wish to express my personal interest in the process for beatification of this good and faithful servant of Christ and the Church. I shall follow with close attention whatever progress may be made in this regard.[60]

The sainted Pope wrote twice to mark the centenary of the death of Cardinal Newman. The first was on April 27, 1990, to the participants in the Academic Symposium that the International Community "The Work" ("Das Werk Gottes") and the Centre of Newman Friends held to commemorate the historic event. He spoke about the vital relevance of Newman's writings to the contemporary world and to Vatican II. He ended his address by calling him "Lover of Truth." He wrote:

> 1. I am very pleased that this meeting allows me to take part as it were in the Academic Symposium which the International Community "The Work" and the Centre of Newman Friends have organized to commemorate the centenary of the death of the renowned Cardinal John Henry Newman. I welcome all of you and thank you for drawing attention through your celebration to the great English Cardinal's special place in the history of the Church. The passage of a hundred years since his death has done nothing to diminish the importance of this extraordinary figure, many of whose ideas enjoy a particular relevance in our own day. The theme

60 John Paul II, "Letter to the Archbishop of Birmingham for the Centenary of the Elevation to the Cardinalate of John Henry Newman," April 7, 1979.

of your Symposium, "John Henry Newman — Lover of Truth," points to a major reason for the continuing attraction of Newman's life and writings. His was a lifelong pursuit of the Truth which alone can make men free (cf. John 8:32).

2. In this brief encounter I can mention only some of the many lessons which Newman holds out to the Church and to the world of culture. I would underline the inspiration that scholars and thoughtful readers of Newman continue to receive today from this pilgrim for truth. . . . Not least among his merits, he reminds us of the need for an interior disposition of loving obedience to God if contemporary society is to be successful in its quest for the full liberating truth which it urgently needs, and indeed knows itself to need.

Ever since his first "conversion grace" at the age of fifteen, Newman was never to lose his sense of God's presence, his respect for revealed truth and his thirst for holiness of life. In his own lifetime, the example of his singular piety and integrity was widely esteemed throughout England by both Catholics and Anglicans alike. His reputation as a man of deep spirituality as well as of learning was one of the principal motives inspiring the English laity to petition Pope Leo XIII to raise the founder of the English Oratory to the College of Cardinals (Cfr. *Letters and Diaries of John Henry Newman*, XXIX, Oxford 1961 ss., 85).

3. Newman's intellectual and spiritual pilgrimage was made in earnest response to an inner light of which he

seemed always aware, the light which conscience projects on all of life's movements and endeavors. For Newman, conscience was a "messenger from Him, who, both in nature and in grace, speaks to us behind a veil" (*Difficulties of Anglicans*, Westminster, Md., II, 248). It inevitably led him to obedience to the authority of the Church, first in the Anglican Communion, and later as a Catholic. His preaching and writings reflected his own lived experience. So, he could instruct his listeners: "Do but examine your thoughts and doings; do but attempt what you know to be God's will, and you will most assuredly be led on into all the truth: you will recognize the force, meaning and awful graciousness of the Gospel Creed..." (*Parochial and Plain Sermons*, VIII, 120).

Newman did not seek worldly success for his own sake, nor did he let the misunderstanding which often accompanied his efforts distract him from the search for true holiness, which was always his conscious aim. He enjoyed great influence and authority during his life, not for any office that he held but because of the human and spiritual personality which he portrayed.

4. The inner drama which marked his long life hinged on the question of holiness and union with Christ. His overriding desire was to know and to do God's will. Thus, at a time of intense spiritual questioning, before retiring to pray about his decision to enter the Catholic Church, he asked his parishioners at Littlemore to "remember such a one in time to come, though you hear him not, and pray for him, that in all things he

may know God's will, and at all times he may be ready to fulfil it" (*Sermons bearing on Subjects of the Day*, Westminster, Md., 1968, 409).

This ideal sustained him in the difficult hour when he sacrificed so much in leaving his beloved and familiar Church of England in order to enter the Catholic Church. His reasoned fidelity to the way God's Providence led him made this experience — what he called the "hidden years" of his life — a source of encouragement and inspiration for many who were looking for the "port after a rough sea" (*Apologia pro Vita Sua*, London 1888, 238). With letters of spiritual direction and counsel he helped countless others along the path of the truth he himself had found and which filled him with so much joy. Newman's influence in this sense has increased over the past hundred years and is no longer limited to England. All over the world people claim that this master of the spirit, by his works, by his example, by his intercession, has been an instrument of divine Providence in their lives.

5. In the contemporary cultural climate, with particular reference to Europe, there is an area of Newman's thought which deserves special attention. I refer to the unity which he advocates between theology and science, between the world of faith and the world of reason. He proposed that learning should not lack unity, but be rooted in a total view. Thus, he concluded his Discourses before the University of Dublin with these striking words: "I wish the intellect to range with the utmost freedom, and religion to enjoy an

equal freedom, but what I am stipulating for is, that they should be found in one and the same place, and exemplified in the same persons" (*Sermons Preached on Various Occasions*, London 1904, 13).

In the present changing circumstances of European culture, does Newman not indicate the essential Christian contribution to building a new era based on a deeper truth and higher values? He wrote: "I want to destroy that diversity of centers, which puts everything into confusion by creating a contrariety of influences. I wish the same spots and the same individuals to be at once oracles of philosophy and shrines of devotion..." (Ibid.). In this endeavor the path the Church must follow is succinctly expressed by the English Cardinal in this way: "The Church fears no knowledge, but she purifies all: she represses no element of our nature, but cultivates the whole" (*The Idea of a University*, Westminster, Md., 234).

6. Still another area of Newman's spiritual itinerary stands out as particularly relevant in the wake of the Second Vatican Council. Because of it we feel Newman to be our true spiritual contemporary. The mystery of the Church always remained the great love of John Henry Newman's life. And in this there is a further profound lesson for the present. Newman's writings project an eminently clear picture of his unwavering love of the Church as the continuing outpouring of God's love for man in every phase of history. His was a truly spiritual vision, capable of perceiving all the weaknesses present in the human fabric

> of the Church, but equally sure in its perception of the mystery hidden beyond our material gaze. May his memory inspire us to make our own the significant prayer that flowed so naturally from his heart: "Let me never forget that Thou hast established on earth a kingdom of Thy own, that the Church is Thy work, Thy establishment, Thy instrument: that we are under Thy rule, Thy laws and Thy eye—that when the Church speaks Thou dost speak. Let not familiarity with this wonderful truth lend me to be insensible to it—let not the weakness of Thy human representatives lead me to forget that it is Thou who dost speak and act through them" (*Meditations and Devotions*, Westminster, Md., 378–379).
>
> 7. May these same sentiments fill all our hearts as we commemorate this eminent churchman. In Newman's entire experience we hear the echo of the words of Jesus to Nicodemus: "He who does what is true comes to the light, that it may be clearly seen that his deeds have been wrought in God" (John 3:21). I trust that your Symposium will inspire further studies to bring out more clearly the importance and relevance of this "Lover of Truth" for our times.[61]

Later that year, on June 18, 1990, Pope John Paul wrote a long letter to Archbishop Maurice Noël Léon Couve de Murville of Birmingham, England. He made a number of references to the relationship between

[61] John Paul II, "Address to the Participants in the Academic Symposium Organized to Commemorate the Centenary of the Death of Cardinal John Henry Newman," April 27, 1990.

the cardinal's life and writings and the teachings of Vatican II, calling him a point of reference for over a hundred years. He wrote:

> 1. At the approach of the first Centenary of the death of John Henry Newman and in response to your kind invitation, I gladly associate myself with the celebrations that mark this event in England and indeed in many countries throughout the world. The memory of the great Cardinal's noble life and his copious writings seem to touch the minds and hearts of many people today with a freshness and relevance that has scarcely faded with the passing of a century.
>
> The Centenary year coincides with the beginning of a period of profound change in world events.... To all searching minds in this present historical context, Newman's voice speaks with a timely message.
>
> 2. Newman's long life shows him to have been an ardent disciple of truth. The unfolding of his career confirms the single-heartedness of his aims as expressed in the following words which he made his own: "My desire hath been to have Truth for my chiefest friend, and no enemy but error" (*The Via Media*, London 1911, Vol. 1, pp. xii-xiii). In periods of trial and suffering he persevered with confidence, knowing that time was on the side of truth.
>
> Newman's quest for the truth led him to search for a voice that would speak to him the authority of the living Christ. His example holds a lasting appeal for all sincere scholars and disciples of truth. He urges them to keep asking the deeper, more basic questions about the

meaning of life and of all human history; not to be content with a partial response to the great mystery that is man himself; to have the intellectual honesty and moral courage to accept the light of truth, no matter what personal sacrifice it may involve. Above all, Newman is a magnificent guide for all those who perceive that the key, the focal point and the goal of all human history is to be found in Christ (cf. *Gaudium et Spes,* 10) and in union with him in that community of faith, hope and charity, which is his holy Church, through which he communicates truth and grace to all (cf. *Lumen Gentium,* 8).

3. Closely connected with this call is John Henry Newman's teaching on the importance of conscience as a means to the acquisition of truth. His doctrine on conscience, like his teaching in general, is subtle and whole, and ought not to be oversimplified in its presentation. He sets out from the basic affirmation that conscience is not simply a sense of propriety, self-respect or good taste, formed by general culture, education and social custom. Rather is it the echo of God's voice within the heart of man, the pulse of the divine law beating within each person as a standard of right and wrong, with an unquestionable authority.

The inner light of conscience puts a person in contact with the reality of a personal God. In one of his books he wrote: "My nature feels towards the voice of conscience as towards a person. When I obey it, I feel a satisfaction; when I disobey, a soreness — just like that which I feel in pleasing or offending some revered friend.... An echo implies a voice; a voice a speaker.

That speaker I love and revere" (*Callista,* London 1910, 314–315).

Moreover, according to Newman, religious obedience to this inner voice puts a person on the look-out for a divine revelation, leads from light to light and ultimately to Christian faith. "Obedience to conscience leads to obedience to the Gospel, which, instead of being something different altogether, is but the completion and perfection of that religion which natural conscience teaches" (*Parochial and Plain Sermons,* London 1908, Vol. VIII, 202).

4. One of Cardinal Newman's lasting merits, in fact, is his struggle to make clear and uphold the vital principle that revealed religion, with its content of doctrine and morals, is the bearer of objective truths which can be known with certitude and assented to with joy and ease (cf. *Dei Verbum,* 5). Few people championed the full rights of conscience as he did; few writers pleaded so persuasively on behalf of its authority and liberty, yet he never allowed any trace of subjectivism or relativism to taint his teaching.

For this reason he taught that although conscience is within the human heart before it receives any training, it is still the duty of a Christian to inform and educate it through the guidance of an authority in order to bring it to maturity and perfection. Left to itself and disregarded, it can become a counterfeit of the sacred power it is, and turn into a kind of self-confidence and deference to a person's own subjective judgment. Newman's words are unequivocal and perennially valid: "Conscience has its rights because it has its duties" (*Difficulties Felt by Anglicans*, London 1910, Vol. II, 250).

5. By following the light of his conscience, Newman made a journey of faith which he has described with force and clarity in his writings. After spending the first half of his life in generous service to the Church of England which he deeply loved, he spent the second half in the service of the Catholic Church, showing a like sincerity and unflinching loyalty. The thoughts and convictions which gave rise to his conversion found their roots and inspiration in the writings of the Fathers of the Church, which are the common patrimony of all Christians. I have often urged that Christians need to rediscover together their common heritage of faith if we are to see the reintegration of Christ's followers in the unity for which he prayed. This is a process that can be remarkably furthered by attention to the work of Newman.

   It was characteristic of him to be firmly faithful to the truth once grasped, while being always ready to develop and deepen his understanding of the deposit of faith. It might be added, moreover, that he combined fidelity to the truth with an attitude of respect and receptivity to the ideas and testimony of those with whom he disagreed. Both in his person and in his work, therefore, Cardinal Newman illuminates the ecumenical journey that we undertake in obedience to the will of Christ (cf. Jn. 17:21). His life and witness furnish us today with a vital resource for understanding and carrying forward the ecumenical movement which has developed so richly in the century since his death.

6. It is my fervent hope that the present Centenary year will occasion in the minds of many people who thirst for truth and genuine freedom a renewed awareness of the lessons to be gained from the life and writings of this outstanding Englishman, priest and cardinal. A man of such consistent loyalty and sincerity could not fail to inspire and draw many others towards the ideal he faithfully served.

Not all agreed with the momentous decisions he took or with the religious principles he advocated, but all unfailingly testified to the spiritual influence his example wielded over others. Some called him their guide in the paths of holiness; others were swayed by the silent force of his humble and withdrawn ways; still others found comfort and peace in his simple exposition of truth; while all were struck by his life of constant prayer and study, and by his familiarity in faith with the "things that are above" (Col. 3:1).

Down to the present day, Newman remains for many a point of reference in a troubled world. They look to him as a man of great natural talent who put every ounce of it at the service of God and the Church. His remarkable life, void of sham and ambition, but steeped in a prayerful communion with the Unseen, while it remained alive to the problems of his age in Church and society, continues to inspire, to uplift and to enlighten.

May the Centenary celebrations issue in abundant grace and spiritual vigor for the Church in England, for your own Archdiocese and for the members of the

> English Congregation of the Oratory of St. Philip Neri, founded by John Henry Newman.[62]

Pope John Paul II published his encyclical *Veritatis Splendor* on August 6, 1993. It states very clearly the position of the Roman Catholic Church regarding fundamentals of the Church's role in moral teaching. The encyclical is truly extraordinary because it is one of the most comprehensive and philosophical teachings on moral theology in the Catholic tradition. The Pope made a reference to Cardinal Newman's writings on the role of conscience in paragraph 34:

> "Teacher, what good must I do to have eternal life?" *The question of morality,* to which Christ provides the answer, *cannot prescind from the issue of freedom. Indeed, it considers that issue central,* for there can be no morality without freedom: "It is only in freedom that man can turn to what is good." *But what sort of freedom?* The Council, considering our contemporaries who "highly regard" freedom and "assiduously pursue" it, but who "often cultivate it in wrong ways as a license to do anything they please, even evil," speaks of *"genuine" freedom*: "Genuine freedom is an outstanding manifestation of the divine image in man. For God willed to leave man "in the power of his own counsel" (cf. Sir. 15:14), so that he would seek his Creator of his own accord and would freely arrive at full and blessed perfection by cleaving to God" (cf. Second Vatican Ecumenical Council, Pastoral Constitution on the Church in the Modern World *Gaudium et Spes,* 17). Although each individual has

[62] John Paul II, "Letter to the Archbishop of Birmingham on the First Centenary of the Death of John Henry Newman," June 18, 1990.

> a right to be respected in his own journey in search of the truth, there exists a prior moral obligation, and a grave one at that, to seek the truth and to adhere to it once it is known (Second Vatican Ecumenical Council, Declaration on Religious Freedom *Dignitatis Humanae,* 2). As Cardinal John Henry Newman, that outstanding defender of the rights of conscience, forcefully put it: "Conscience has rights because it has duties" (*A Letter Addressed to His Grace the Duke of Norfolk: Certain Difficulties Felt by Anglicans in Catholic Teaching* [Uniform Edition: Longman, Green and Company, London,1868–1881], vol. 2, 250).[63]

The Pope sent a letter to Archbishop Vincent Nichols of Birmingham, England,[64] on January 22, 2001, to mark the second centenary of the birth of Cardinal Newman. He spoke about the cardinal's distinct gifts and witness to the Catholic Church, which endure beyond his death, and of his conviction that God had given him a specific mission which he faithfully fulfilled. He wrote:

> On the occasion of the second centenary of the birth of the Venerable Servant of God John Henry Newman, I gladly join you, your Brother Bishops of England and Wales, the priests of the Birmingham Oratory and a host of voices throughout the world in praising God for the gift of the great English Cardinal and for his enduring witness.
>
> As Newman pondered the mysterious divine plan unfolding in his own life, he came to a deep and abiding sense that "God has created me to do Him some definite service.

[63] John Paul II, Encyclical Letter *Veritatis Splendor* (August 6, 1993).

[64] He is the current Archbishop of Westminster and a cardinal.

He has committed some work to me which he has not committed to another. I have my mission" (*Meditations and Devotions*). How true that thought now appears as we consider his long life and the influence which he has had beyond death.... The particular mission entrusted to him by God ensures that John Henry Newman belongs to every time and place and people.

Newman was born in troubled times which knew not only political and military upheaval but also turbulence of soul. Old certitudes were shaken, and believers were faced with the threat of rationalism on the one hand and fideism on the other. Rationalism brought with it a rejection of both authority and transcendence, while fideism turned from the challenges of history and the tasks of this world to a distorted dependence upon authority and the supernatural. In such a world, Newman came eventually to a remarkable synthesis of faith and reason which were for him "like two wings on which the human spirit rises to the contemplation of the truth" (*Fides et Ratio*, Introduction; cf. ibid., 74). It was the passionate contemplation of truth which also led him to a liberating acceptance of the authority which has its roots in Christ, and to the sense of the supernatural which opens the human mind and heart to the full range of possibilities revealed in Christ. "Lead kindly light amid the encircling gloom, lead Thou me on," Newman wrote in *The Pillar of the Cloud*; and for him Christ was the light at the heart of every kind of darkness. For his tomb he chose the inscription: *Ex umbris et imaginibus in veritatem*; and it was clear at the end of his life's journey that Christ was the truth he had found.

But Newman's search was shot through with pain. Once he had come to that unshakeable sense of the mission entrusted to him by God, he declared: "Therefore, I will trust Him.... If I am in sickness, my sickness may serve Him, in perplexity, my perplexity may serve Him.... He does nothing in vain.... He may take away my friends. He may throw me among strangers. He may make me feel desolate, make my spirits sink, hide the future from me. Still, He knows what He is about" (*Meditations and Devotions*). All these trials he knew in his life; but rather than diminish or destroy him they paradoxically strengthened his faith in the God who had called him, and confirmed him in the conviction that God "does nothing in vain." In the end, therefore, what shines forth in Newman is the mystery of the Lord's Cross: this was the heart of his mission, the absolute truth which he contemplated, the "kindly light" which led him on.

... We pray that this sure and eloquent guide in our perplexity will also become for us in all our needs a powerful intercessor before the throne of grace. Let us pray that the time will soon come when the Church can officially and publicly proclaim the exemplary holiness of Cardinal John Henry Newman, one of the most distinguished and versatile champions of English spirituality.[65]

Pope Benedict XVI

Cardinal Joseph Ratzinger was the Prefect of the Congregation (now called Dicastery) for the Doctrine of the Faith when he was elected to succeed Pope John Paul II on April 19, 2005. He took the name Pope Benedict XVI (2005–resigned, 2013), expecting his pontificate to be brief. It is no secret that Pope Benedict XVI was an unabashed great admirer of

[65] John Paul II, "Letter on the Occasion of the 2nd Centenary of the Birth of Cardinal John Henry Newman," January 22, 2001.

Cardinal Newman, dating back to his years as a seminarian. In fact, as already stated, they both valued the preeminence of conscience.

Joseph Ratzinger was born in Bavaria, Germany, on April 16, 1927. Soon after he was ordained a priest on June 29, 1951 (along with his older brother, Georg), he embarked on an academic career. He soon established himself as a highly respected theologian, being appointed a professor at the tender age of thirty-one. Though he lacked a good pastoral experience, Pope Paul VI appointed him as Archbishop of Munich and Freising in 1977. Pope John Paul II appointed him Prefect of the Congregation for the Doctrine of the Faith in 1981. He remained in that capacity until his papal election in 2005. Cardinal Ratzinger was one of Pope John Paul II's closest collaborators and one of his most intimate confidants. It was stated many times that his influence during the papacy of John Paul II was second to none in matters that involved Church priorities and direction.[66]

No one questions the fact that he was a prolific writer, even when Pope, and his interests and expertise were multiple. He was one of the most brilliant Popes to occupy the Chair of St. Peter. The day before the conclave that elected him Pope, *Time* magazine identified him as one of the one hundred most influential people in the world.[67] He took the entire world by surprise when, on February 11, 2013, he announced that he was going to resign the papacy the following February 28. He was the first Pope who willingly stepped down since Pope Gregory XII in 1451. Benedict XVI, as Pope emeritus, stayed at Castel Gandolfo until the Mater Ecclesiae Monastery

[66] Mary Ann Walsh, *From Pope John Paul II to Benedict XVI: An Inside Look at the End of an Era, the Beginning of a New One, and the Future of the Church* (Rowman and Littlefield, 2005), 135.

[67] Andrew Sullivan, "Joseph Cardinal Ratzinger," (The 2005 TIME 100), *Time*, April 18, 2005, https://content.time.com/time/specials/packages/article/0,28804,1972656_1972691_1973018,00.html.

within the Vatican Gardens was turned into his permanent residence. He moved there on May 2, 2013. At the time of his death inside the convent, on December 31, 2022, he was the last cardinal appointed by Pope Paul VI to die.[68]

Pope Benedict XVI spoke about Cardinal Newman on a number of occasions during 2010. While speaking with the bishops of the Episcopal Conference of England and Wales during their *ad limina* visit on February 1, 2010, he presented Cardinal Newman as a great example to be emulated by priests:

> It is the truth revealed through Scripture and Tradition and articulated by the Church's Magisterium that sets us free. Cardinal Newman realized this, and he left us an outstanding example of faithfulness to revealed truth by following that "kindly light" wherever it led him, even at considerable personal cost. Great writers and communicators of his stature and integrity are needed in the Church today, and it is my hope that devotion to him will inspire many to follow in his footsteps.
>
> Much attention has rightly been given to Newman's scholarship and to his extensive writings, but it is important to remember that he saw himself first and foremost as a priest. In this *Annus Sacerdotalis*, I urge you to hold up to your priests his example of dedication to prayer, pastoral sensitivity towards the needs of his flock, and passion for preaching the Gospel. You yourselves should set a similar example.... In Newman's words, "Christ's priests have no priesthood but His ... what they do, He does; when they

[68] Pope Paul VI named him cardinal priest of Santa Maria Consolatrice al Tiburtino during the consistory of June 27, 1977.

> baptize, He is baptizing; when they bless, He is blessing" (*Parochial and Plain Sermons*, VI 242).[69]

In his greetings during the Wednesday General Audience of September 8, 2010, Benedict XVI spoke about the upcoming Beatification of Cardinal Newman:

> It will be a particular joy for me to beatify the Venerable John Henry Newman in Birmingham on Sunday 19 September. This truly great Englishman lived an exemplary priestly life and through his extensive writings made a lasting contribution to Church and society both in his native land and in many other parts of the world. It is my hope and prayer that more and more people will benefit from his gentle wisdom and be inspired by his example of integrity and holiness of life.[70]

Soon thereafter, Pope Benedict XVI spoke extensively during his flight from Rome to Britain on September 16, 2010. He described Newman's entire life as a journey in search of truth. He took questions from various journalists on the flight. One of the journalists, Fr. Lombardi, asked the following:

> Your Holiness, Cardinal Newman is obviously very important for you. For Cardinal Newman you are making an exception by presiding at his beatification. Are you of the opinion that recalling him can help to overcome divisions

69 Benedict XVI, "Address to the Bishops of the Episcopal Conference of England and Wales on Their 'Ad Limina' Visit," February 1, 2010.

70 Benedict XVI, General Audience, September 8, 2010.

between Anglicans and Catholics? Also, what aspects of his personality do you intend to stress more?

The Pope responded this way:

> On the one hand Cardinal Newman was above all a modern man, who lived the whole problem of modernity; he faced the problem of agnosticism, the impossibility of knowing God, of believing. He was a man whose whole life was a journey, a journey in which he allowed himself to be transformed by truth in a search marked by great sincerity and great openness, so as to know better and to find and accept the path that leads to true life. This interior modernity, in his being and in his life, demonstrates the modernity of his faith. It is not a faith of formulas of past ages; it is a very personal faith, a faith lived, suffered and found in a long path of renewal and conversion. He was a man of great culture, who on the other hand shared in our skeptical culture of today, in the question whether we can know something for certain regarding the truth of man and his being, and how we can come to convergent probabilities. He was a man with a great culture and knowledge of the Fathers of the Church. He studied and renewed the interior genesis of faith and recognized its inner form and construction. He was a man of great spirituality, of humanity, of prayer, with a profound relationship with God, a personal relationship, and hence a deep relationship with the people of his time and ours. So I would point to these three elements: modernity in his life with the same doubts and problems of our lives today; his great culture, his knowledge of the treasures of human culture, openness to permanent search, to permanent renewal and, spirituality,

> spiritual life, life with God; these elements give to this man an exceptional stature for our time. That is why he is like a Doctor of the Church for us and for all, and also a bridge between Anglicans and Catholics.[71]

Among the papal activities while in England to beatify Cardinal Newman was a fraternal visit on September 17, 2010, to Lambeth Palace, the residence of Anglican Archbishop Rowan Williams of Canterbury. Pope Benedict said:

> In the figure of John Henry Newman, who is to be beatified on Sunday, we celebrate a churchman whose ecclesial vision was nurtured by his Anglican background and matured during his many years of ordained ministry in the Church of England. He can teach us the virtues that ecumenism demands: on the one hand, he was moved to follow his conscience, even at great personal cost; and on the other hand, the warmth of his continued friendship with his former colleagues, led him to explore with them, in a truly eirenical spirit, the questions on which they differed, driven by a deep longing for unity in faith. Your Grace, in that same spirit of friendship, let us renew our determination to pursue the goal of unity in faith, hope, and love, in accordance with the will of our one Lord and Savior Jesus Christ.[72]

[71] Benedict XVI, Interview with the Journalists During the Flight to the United Kingdom, Apostolic Journey to the United Kingdom, September 16, 2010.

[72] Benedict XVI, "Address During Visit to the Archbishop of Canterbury," Lambeth Palace, September 17, 2010.

A prayer vigil on the eve of the cardinal's Beatification took place in Hyde Park, London, on September 18, 2010. The Pope delivered an address for the occasion. He publicly acknowledged that Newman had an important influence in his life and thoughts. He spoke about Newman's prophetic vision of the role of the laity in the Church. He described his personal joy of beatifying the cardinal, as well as the joy of many people across the world, and afterward would continue to speak about his joy in beatifying Newman.

> This is an evening of joy, of immense spiritual joy, for all of us. We are gathered here in prayerful vigil to prepare for tomorrow's Mass, during which a great son of this nation, Cardinal John Henry Newman, will be declared Blessed. How many people, in England and throughout the world, have longed for this moment! It is also a great joy for me, personally, to share this experience with you. As you know, Newman has long been an important influence in my own life and thought, as he has been for so many people beyond these isles. The drama of Newman's life invites us to examine our lives, to see them against the vast horizon of God's plan, and to grow in communion with the Church of every time and place: the Church of the apostles, the Church of the martyrs, the Church of the saints, the Church which Newman loved and to whose mission he devoted his entire life
>
> . . . I would like to reflect with you about a few aspects of Newman's life which I consider very relevant to our lives as believers and to the life of the Church today.
>
> Let me begin by recalling that Newman, by his own account, traced the course of his whole life back to a powerful experience of conversion which he had as a young man. It was an immediate experience of the truth of God's word,

of the objective reality of Christian revelation as handed down in the Church. This experience, at once religious and intellectual, would inspire his vocation to be a minister of the Gospel, his discernment of the source of authoritative teaching in the Church of God, and his zeal for the renewal of ecclesial life in fidelity to the apostolic tradition. At the end of his life, Newman would describe his life's work as a struggle against the growing tendency to view religion as a purely private and subjective matter, a question of personal opinion. Here is the first lesson we can learn from his life: in our day, when an intellectual and moral relativism threatens to sap the very foundations of our society, Newman reminds us that, as men and women made in the image and likeness of God, we were created to know the truth, to find in that truth our ultimate freedom and the fulfilment of our deepest human aspirations. In a word, we are meant to know Christ, who is himself "the way, and the truth, and the life" (John 14:16).

Newman's life also teaches us that passion for the truth, intellectual honesty and genuine conversion are costly. The truth that sets us free cannot be kept to ourselves; it calls for testimony, it begs to be heard, and in the end its convincing power comes from itself and not from the human eloquence or arguments in which it may be couched. . . .

Finally, Newman teaches us that if we have accepted the truth of Christ and committed our lives to him, there can be no separation between what we believe and the way we live our lives. Our every thought, word and action must be directed to the glory of God and the spread of his Kingdom. Newman understood this, and was the great champion of the prophetic office of the Christian laity. He saw clearly that we do not so much accept the truth in a purely intellectual act as embrace it in a spiritual dynamic that penetrates to the core of our being. Truth is passed on not merely by formal teaching, important as that is, but also by the witness of lives lived in integrity, fidelity and holiness; those who live in and by the truth instinctively recognize what is false and, precisely as false, inimical to the beauty and goodness which accompany the splendor of truth, *veritatis splendor*.

... Through faith we come to see God's word as a lamp for our steps and light for our path (cf. Ps. 119:105). Newman, like the countless saints who preceded him along the path of Christian discipleship, taught that the "kindly light" of faith leads us to realize the truth about ourselves, our dignity as God's children, and the sublime destiny which awaits us in heaven.... Without the life of prayer, without the interior transformation which takes place through the grace of the sacraments, we cannot, in Newman's words, "radiate Christ"; we become just another "clashing cymbal" (1 Cor. 13:1) in a world filled with growing noise and confusion, filled with false paths leading only to heartbreak and illusion.

One of the Cardinal's best-loved meditations includes the words, "God has created me to do him some definite service. He has committed some work to me which he has not committed to another" (*Meditations on Christian Doctrine*). Here we see Newman's fine Christian realism, the point at which faith and life inevitably intersect. Faith is meant to bear fruit in the transformation of our world through the power of the Holy Spirit at work in the lives and activity of believers. No one who looks realistically at our world today could think that Christians can afford to go on with business as usual, ignoring the profound crisis of faith which has overtaken our society, or simply trusting that the patrimony of values handed down by the Christian centuries will continue to inspire and shape the future of our society. We know that in times of crisis and upheaval God has raised up great saints and prophets for the renewal of the Church and Christian society; we trust in his providence and we pray for his continued guidance. But each of us, in accordance with his or her state of life, is called to work for the advancement of God's Kingdom by imbuing temporal life with the values of the Gospel. Each of us has a mission, each of us is called to change the world, to work for a culture of life, a culture forged by love and respect for the dignity of each human person. As our Lord tells us in the Gospel we have just heard, our light must shine in the sight of all, so that, seeing our good works, they may give praise to our heavenly Father (cf. Mt. 5:16)....

... Let us continue our vigil of prayer by preparing to encounter Christ, present among us in the Blessed Sacrament of the Altar. Together, in the silence of our common adoration, let us open our minds and hearts to his presence, his love, and the convincing power of his truth. In a special way, let us thank him for the enduring witness to that truth offered by Cardinal John Henry Newman. Trusting in his prayers, let us ask the Lord to illumine our path, and the path of all British society, with the kindly light of his truth, his love and his peace. Amen.[73]

73 Benedict XVI, "Address at Prayer Vigil on the Eve of the Beatification of Cardinal John Henry Newman," Hyde Park, London, September 18, 2010.

During the Beatification Mass of Cardinal John Henry Newman, Pope Benedict XVI gave a masterful and passionate homily about the new Blessed, including also some personal experiences. The Mass was celebrated at Cofton Park of Rednal, Birmingham, England, on September 19, 2010. He stated:

> This day that has brought us together here in Birmingham is a most auspicious one.... It is the day that sees Cardinal John Henry Newman formally raised to the altars and declared Blessed.
>
> ... I thank you for your presence at this celebration, in which we give glory and praise to God for the heroic virtue of a saintly Englishman.
>
> England has a long tradition of martyr saints, whose courageous witness has sustained and inspired the Catholic community here for centuries. Yet it is right and fitting that we should recognize today the holiness of a confessor, a son of this nation who, while not called to shed his blood for the Lord, nevertheless bore eloquent witness to him in the course of a long life devoted to the priestly ministry, and especially to preaching, teaching, and writing.... In Blessed John Henry, that tradition of gentle scholarship, deep human wisdom and profound love for the Lord has borne rich fruit, as a sign of the abiding presence of the Holy Spirit deep within the heart of God's people, bringing forth abundant gifts of holiness.
>
> Cardinal Newman's motto, *Cor ad cor loquitur*, or "Heart speaks unto heart," gives us an insight into his understanding of the Christian life as a call to holiness, experienced as the profound desire of the human heart to enter into intimate communion with the Heart of God. He reminds us that

faithfulness to prayer gradually transforms us into the divine likeness. As he wrote in one of his many fine sermons, "a habit of prayer, the practice of turning to God and the unseen world in every season, in every place, in every emergency — prayer, I say, has what may be called a natural effect in spiritualizing and elevating the soul. A man is no longer what he was before; gradually ... he has imbibed a new set of ideas, and become imbued with fresh principles" (*Parochial and Plain Sermons*, iv, 230–231). Today's Gospel tells us that no one can be the servant of two masters (cf. Lk. 16:13), and Blessed John Henry's teaching on prayer explains how the faithful Christian is definitively taken into the service of the one true Master, who alone has a claim to our unconditional devotion (cf. Mt. 23:10). Newman helps us to understand what this means for our daily lives: he tells us that our divine Master has assigned a specific task to each one of us, a "definite service," committed uniquely to every single person: "I have my mission," he wrote, "I am a link in a chain, a bond of connection between persons. He has not created me for naught. I shall do good, I shall do his work; I shall be an angel of peace, a preacher of truth in my own place ... if I do but keep his commandments and serve him in my calling" (*Meditations and Devotions*, 301–2).

The definite service to which Blessed John Henry was called involved applying his keen intellect and his prolific pen to many of the most pressing "subjects of the day." His insights into the relationship between faith and reason, into the vital place of revealed religion in civilized society, and into the need for a broadly-based and wide-ranging approach to education were not only of profound importance for Victorian England, but continue today to inspire and enlighten many all over the world. I would like to pay particular tribute to his vision for education, which has done so much to shape the ethos that is the driving force behind Catholic schools and colleges today. Firmly opposed to any reductive or utilitarian approach, he sought to achieve an educational environment in which intellectual training, moral discipline and religious commitment would come together. The project to found a Catholic University in Ireland provided him with an opportunity to develop his ideas on the subject, and the collection of discourses that he published as *The Idea of a University* holds up an ideal from which all those engaged in academic formation can continue to learn. And indeed, what better goal could teachers of religion set themselves than Blessed John Henry's famous appeal for an intelligent, well-instructed laity: "I want a laity, not arrogant, not rash in speech, not disputatious, but men who know their religion, who enter into it, who know just where they stand, who know what they hold and what they do not, who know their creed so well that they can give an account of it, who know so much of history that they can defend it" (*The Present Position of Catholics in England*, ix, 390). On this day when the author of those words is raised to the altars, I pray that, through his intercession and example, all who are engaged in the task of teaching and catechesis will be inspired to greater effort by the vision he so clearly sets before us.

While it is John Henry Newman's intellectual legacy that has understandably received most attention in the vast literature devoted to his life and work, I prefer on this occasion to conclude with a brief reflection on his life as a priest, a pastor of souls. The warmth and humanity underlying his appreciation of the pastoral ministry is beautifully expressed in another of his famous sermons: "Had Angels been your priests, my brethren, they could not have condoled with you, sympathized with you, have had compassion on you, felt tenderly for you, and made allowances for you, as we can; they could not have been your patterns and guides, and have led you on from your old selves into a new life, as they can who come from the midst of you" ("Men, not Angels: the Priests of the Gospel," *Discourses to Mixed Congregations*, 3). He lived out that profoundly human vision of priestly ministry in his devoted care for the people of Birmingham during the years that he spent at the Oratory he founded, visiting the sick and the poor, comforting the bereaved, caring for those in prison. No wonder that on his death so many thousands of people lined the local streets as his body was taken to its place of burial not half a mile from here. One hundred and twenty years later, great crowds have assembled once again to rejoice in the Church's solemn recognition of the outstanding holiness of this much-loved father of souls. What better way to express the joy of this moment than by turning to our heavenly Father in heartfelt thanksgiving, praying in the words that Blessed John Henry Newman placed on the lips of the choirs of angels in heaven:

Praise to the Holiest in the height
And in the depth be praise;
In all his words most wonderful,
Most sure in all his ways!
(*The Dream of Gerontius*)[74]

74 Benedict XVI, "Homily at Mass with the Beatification of Venerable Cardinal John Henry Newman," Cofton Park of Rednal, Birmingham, September 19, 2010.

The *Angelus* followed the Mass of Beatification in the same park. The Pope spoke about Blessed John Henry Newman's devotion and love for the Blessed Virgin — he had been a Marian devotee.

> When Blessed John Henry Newman came to live in Birmingham, he gave the name "Maryvale" to his first home here. The Oratory that he founded is dedicated to the Immaculate Conception of the Blessed Virgin. And the Catholic University of Ireland he placed under the patronage of Mary, *Sedes Sapientiae*. In so many ways, he lived his priestly ministry in a spirit of filial devotion to the Mother of God. Meditating upon her role in the unfolding of God's plan for our salvation, he was moved to exclaim: "Who can estimate the holiness and perfection of her, who was chosen to be the Mother of Christ? What must have been her gifts, who was chosen to be the only near earthly relative of the Son of God, the only one whom He was bound by nature to revere and look up to; the one appointed to train and educate Him, to instruct Him day by day, as He grew in wisdom and in stature?" (*Parochial and Plain Sermons*, ii, 131–2). It is on account of those abundant gifts of grace that we honor her, and it is on account of that intimacy with her divine Son that we naturally seek her intercession for our own needs and the needs of the whole world. In the words of the *Angelus*, we turn now to our Blessed Mother and commend to her the intentions that we hold in our hearts.[75]

[75] Benedict XVI, Angelus, Cofton Park of Rednal, Birmingham, September 19, 2010.

Pope Benedict XVI, back in Rome from Britain, spoke about his experience of the event of the Beatification of Cardinal Newman during the Wednesday General Audience of September 22, 2010.

Today I would like to say more about my Apostolic Journey to the United Kingdom which God granted me to make a few days ago.... The main purpose of the Visit was to proclaim blessed Cardinal John Henry Newman, one of the greatest Englishmen in recent times, an outstanding theologian and man of the Church. In fact, the beatification ceremony was the culmination of the Apostolic Journey, whose theme was inspired by the motto Blessed Newman chose on being created a Cardinal: "Heart speaks unto heart." ...

As I was saying, the crowning point of my Visit to the United Kingdom was the Beatification of Cardinal John Henry Newman, an outstanding son of England. It was preceded and prepared for by a special Prayer Vigil that took place on Saturday evening in Hyde Park, London, in an atmosphere of profound recollection. To the multitudes of the faithful, especially young people, I chose to present anew the luminous figure of Cardinal Newman, an intellectual and a believer, whose basic spiritual message testifies that the path to knowledge is not withdrawal into "self," but openness, conversion and obedience to the One who is the Way, the Truth and the Life. The rite of Beatification took place in Birmingham at the solemn Eucharistic celebration on Sunday.... This moving event brought even more into the limelight a scholar of great stature, an outstanding writer and poet, a wise man of God, whose thought illumined many consciences and still today exerts an extraordinary fascination. May believers and ecclesial

> communities in the United Kingdom in particular draw inspiration from him so that, in our day too, this noble land may continue to produce abundant fruits of gospel life....
>
> Blessed John Henry Newman, whose figure and writings still preserve a remarkable timeliness, deserves to be known by all. He supports the resolutions and efforts of Christians to spread everywhere they go the fragrance of Christ, so that their whole life and being may be only his radiance, as he wrote wisely in his booklet *Radiating Christ*.[76]

Pope Benedict XVI, on November 18, 2010, sent a message on the occasion of a symposium organized by the International Centre of Newman Friends. He spoke about Newman's eminent contribution in defense of the truth:

> While the joy of having been able to beatify Cardinal John Henry Newman during my recent visit to the United Kingdom is still alive within me, I address a cordial greeting to you, to the distinguished Relators and to all the participants in the Symposium organized in Rome by the International Centre of Newman Friends. I express my appreciation of the chosen theme: "The Primacy of God in the Life and Writings of Bl. John Henry Newman." This theme rightly emphasizes theocentrism as a fundamental perspective which characterizes the personality and opus of the great English theologian.
>
> It is well known that the young Newman, although he had come to know the "religion of the Bible" thanks to his mother, endured a period in his life full of difficulties and

[76] Benedict XVI, General Audience, September 22, 2010.

doubts. At the age of 14 he was influenced by philosophers such as Hume and Voltaire and, in identifying with their objections to religion, turned towards a kind of deism, in accordance with the humanist and liberal trends of that time.

Nevertheless, in the following year, Newman received the grace of conversion, finding repose "in the thought of two and two only absolute and luminously self-evident beings, myself and my Creator" (J. H. Newman, *Apologia pro vita sua,* Chapter 1. "History of My Religious Opinions to the Year 1833"). He therefore discovered the objective truth of a personal and living God, who speaks to the conscience and reveals to man his condition as a creature. He understood his dependence on the existence of the One, who is the beginning of all things, finding in him the origin and sense of identity and personal uniqueness. It is this particular experience that constitutes the base for the primacy of God in Newman's life.

After his conversion, he was guided by two fundamental criteria — drawn from the book *The Force of Truth* by the Calvinist Thomas Scott — which fully manifest the primacy of God in his life. The first: "Holiness rather than peace" (ibid.), which documents his determination to adhere to the interior Master with his own conscience, confidently abandoning himself to the Father and living in faithfulness to the recognized truth. These ideals were later to entail "a great price to pay." In fact, Newman both as an Anglican and as a Catholic, was subjected to many trials, disappointments and misunderstandings. Yet, he never descended to false compromises or easy agreements. He always remained honest in his search for the truth, faithful to the promptings of his conscience and focused on the ideal of sanctity.

The second motto Newman chose was "Growth is the only evidence of life" (ibid.), which completely expresses his willingness for continuous conversion, transformation and interior growth, always faithfully relying on God. Thus he discovered his vocation in service to the Word of God and, turning to the Fathers of the Church to find greater light, proposed a true reform of Anglicanism, adhering in the end to the Catholic Church. He summed up his own experience of growth in faithfulness to himself and to the Lord's will in these well-known words: "Here below to live is to change, and to be perfect is to have changed often" (J. H. Newman, *An Essay on the Development of Christian Doctrine,* Chapter 1, "On the Development of Ideas"). Newman, during his long life, was one who converted, who was transformed and in this way remained the same, becoming ever more himself.

The horizon of God's primacy also deeply marks Newman's numerous publications. The cited essay on the *Development of Christian Doctrine* states: "That there is a truth then; that there is one truth; ... the search for truth is not the gratification of curiosity; that its attainment has nothing of the excitement of a discovery; that the mind is below truth, not above it, and is bound, not to descant upon it, but to venerate it" (ibid., Chapter 8, "Application of the Third Note of a True Development—Assimilative Power"). The primacy of God is therefore expressed as the primacy of truth, a truth that must be sought first of all by orienting one's interiority to acceptance, in an open and sincere exchange with all, and that finds its culmination in the encounter with Christ "the Way, the Truth, and the Life" (Jn. 14:6). Newman thus bore witness to the Truth also with his very rich literary production, ranging from theology to poetry, from philosophy to pedagogy, from exegesis to the history of Christianity, from novels to meditations and to prayers.

In presenting and defending the Truth, Newman was always careful to find the appropriate language, the correct form and a suitable tone. He tried never to offend others and to witness to the gentle inner light, the "kindly light," forcing himself to convince others with humility, happiness and patience. In a prayer to St. Philip Neri he wrote: "that my countenance may always be open and cheerful, and my words kind and pleasant, as becomes those who, in whatever state of life they are, have the greatest of all goods, the favor of God and the prospect of eternal bliss" (J. H. Newman, *Meditations and Devotions,* Novena of St. Philip May 22, Philip's Cheerfulness).

I entrust to Bl. John Henry Newman, a master in teaching us, that the primacy of God is the primacy of the truth and of love, the reflections and work of this Symposium as, through the intercession of the Virgin Mary, Mother of the Church, I am pleased to impart to you and to all the participants the implored Apostolic Blessing, a pledge of abundant heavenly favours.[77]

Pope Benedict XVI made reference to Blessed Newman in an address to the members of the International Theological Commission on December 3, 2010. He portrayed Newman as one who found the school of sanctity in theology:

[77] Benedict XVI, "Message on the Occasion of the Symposium Organized by the International Centre of Newman Friends," November 18, 2010.

> The consequence of this acceptance and transmission of the Logos is also the fact that the very rationality of theology helps to purify human reason, liberating it from certain prejudices and ideas that can exercise a strong influence on the thought of every age. It should, moreover, be pointed out that theology always lives in a continuity and in a dialogue with the believers and theologians who came before us; since ecclesial communion is diachronic, so also is theology. The theologian never begins from zero, but considers as teachers the Fathers and theologians of the whole Christian tradition. Rooted in Sacred Scripture, read with the Fathers and Doctors, theology can be the school of sanctity, as witnessed by Bl. John Henry Newman. To discover the permanent value of the riches passed down from the past is no small contribution of theology to the symphony of the sciences.[78]

The members of the Roman Curia gathered in the *Sala Regia* on December 20, 2010, to exchange Christmas greetings with Pope Benedict XVI. He ended his greeting by referring to Blessed Newman. He exhibited a great knowledge and profound understanding of Newman and his writings.

> Finally I should like to recall once more the beatification of Cardinal John Henry Newman. Why was he beatified? What does he have to say to us? Many responses could be given to these questions, which were explored in the context of the beatification. I would like to highlight just two aspects which belong together and which, in the final

[78] Benedict XVI, "Address to Members of the International Theological Commission," Consistory Hall, December 3, 2010.

analysis, express the same thing. The first is that we must learn from Newman's three conversions, because they were steps along a spiritual path that concerns us all. Here I would like to emphasize just the first conversion: to faith in the living God. Until that moment, Newman thought like the average men of his time and indeed like the average men of today, who do not simply exclude the existence of God, but consider it as something uncertain, something with no essential role to play in their lives. What appeared genuinely real to him, as to the men of his and our day, is the empirical, matter that can be grasped. This is the "reality" according to which one finds one's bearings. The "real" is what can be grasped, it is the things that can be calculated and taken in one's hand. In his conversion, Newman recognized that it is exactly the other way round: that God and the soul, man's spiritual identity, constitute what is genuinely real, what counts. These are much more real than objects that can be grasped. This conversion was a Copernican revolution. What had previously seemed unreal and secondary was now revealed to be the genuinely decisive element. Where such a conversion takes place, it is not just a person's theory that changes: the fundamental shape of life changes. We are all in constant need of such conversion: then we are on the right path.

The driving force that impelled Newman along the path of conversion was conscience. But what does this mean? In modern thinking, the word "conscience" signifies that for moral and religious questions, it is the subjective dimension, the individual, that constitutes the final authority for decision. The world is divided into the realms of the objective and the subjective. To the objective realm belong things that can be calculated and verified by experiment. Religion and morals fall outside the scope of these methods and are therefore considered to lie within the subjective realm. Here, it is said, there are in the final analysis no objective criteria. The ultimate instance that can decide here is therefore the subject alone, and precisely this is what the word "conscience" expresses: in this realm only the individual, with his intuitions and experiences, can decide. Newman's understanding of conscience is diametrically opposed to this. For him, "conscience" means man's capacity for truth: the capacity to recognize precisely in the decision-making areas of his life — religion and morals — a truth, *the* truth. At the same time, conscience — man's capacity to recognize truth — thereby imposes on him the obligation to set out along the path towards truth, to seek it and to submit to it wherever he finds it. Conscience is both capacity for truth and obedience to the truth which manifests itself to anyone who seeks it with an open heart. The path of Newman's conversions is a path of conscience — not a path of self-asserting subjectivity but, on the contrary, a path of obedience to the truth that was gradually opening up to him. His third conversion, to Catholicism, required him to give up almost everything that was dear and precious to him: possessions, profession, academic rank, family ties and many friends. The sacrifice demanded of him by obedience to the truth, by his conscience, went further still. Newman had always been aware of having a mission for England. But in the Catholic theology of his time, his voice could hardly make itself heard. It was too foreign in the context of the prevailing form of theological thought and devotion. In January 1863 he wrote in his

> diary these distressing words: "As a Protestant, I felt my religion dreary, but not my life — but, as a Catholic, my life dreary, not my religion." He had not yet arrived at the hour when he would be an influential figure. In the humility and darkness of obedience, he had to wait until his message was taken up and understood. In support of the claim that Newman's concept of conscience matched the modern subjective understanding, people often quote a letter in which he said — should he have to propose a toast — that he would drink first to conscience and then to the Pope. But in this statement, "conscience" does not signify the ultimately binding quality of subjective intuition. It is an expression of the accessibility and the binding force of truth: on this its primacy is based. The second toast can be dedicated to the Pope because it is his task to demand obedience to the truth.[79]

Pope Benedict XVI ordained five archbishops in St. Peter's Basilica on February 5, 2011. They were Savio Hon Tai-Fai; Marcello Bartolucci; Celso Morga Iruzubieta; Antonio Guido Filipazzi; and Edgar Peña Parra. He made reference to Blessed Newman's three conversions:

> Cardinal Newman, whose way through life was marked by three conversions, said that living implies transforming oneself. Yet his three conversions and the transformations that occurred in them are one, consistent journey: the

[79] Benedict XVI, "Address on the Occasion of Christmas Greetings to the Roman Curia," Sala Regia, December 20, 2010.

> journey of obedience to the truth, to God; the journey of true continuity which in this very way brings progress.[80]

Ambassadors from any country around the world personally present their formal diplomatic letter, commonly called diplomatic credentials, addressed from one head of state to another. The letter requests acceptance of the ambassador's claim of speaking for the country and the government he or she is representing. All new ambassadors to the Holy See present their country's diplomatic credentials to the Pope. This formal ceremony marks the beginning of the ambassadorship.

Mr. Nigel Marcus Baker, on his forty-fifth birthday, September 9, 2011, formally presented his diplomatic credentials to Pope Benedict XVI. He was the ambassador of the United Kingdom of Great Britain and Northern Ireland to the Holy See. The Pope took the occasion to speak about his visit to that country to beatify the person he greatly admired, Blessed Newman.

> The Holy See and the United Kingdom have enjoyed excellent relations in the thirty years that have passed since full diplomatic relations were established. The close bond between us was further strengthened last year during my Visit to your country, a unique occasion in the course of the shared history of the Holy See and the countries which today compose the United Kingdom. I would therefore like to begin my remarks by reiterating my gratitude to the British people for the warm welcome which I received during my stay. Her Majesty and His Royal Highness the Duke of Edinburgh received me most graciously and I was pleased to meet

[80] Benedict XVI, "Homily at Papal Mass for the Episcopal Ordination of Five Archbishops," Vatican Basilica, February 5, 2011.

> the leaders of the three main political parties and to discuss with them matters of common concern. As you know, a particular motive for my Visit was the Beatification of John Henry Cardinal Newman, a great Englishman whom I have admired for many years and whose raising to the altars was a personal wish fulfilled. I remain convinced of the relevance of Newman's insights regarding society, as the United Kingdom, Europe and the West in general today face challenges that he identified with remarkable prophetic clarity. It is my hope that a fresh awareness of his writings will bear new fruit among those searching for solutions to the political, economic and social questions of our age.[81]

Pope Benedict XVI was a naturally talented teacher, who never stopped teaching, even during his papacy. He spoke to the participants in the World Congress for the Pastoral Care of International Students on December 2, 2011. He referred to Blessed Newman, indicating, without saying so explicitly, how Newman viewed university life.

> The university world is a vital field for the evangelization of the Church. As I pointed out in my Message for the World Day of Migrants and Refugees for next year, when Christian universities are faithful to their true identity, they become places of witness, where Jesus Christ can be met and known, where one can experience his presence, that reconciles, calms, and instills new hope. The spread of "weak" ideologies in the various sectors of society urges Christians to make fresh efforts in the academic world, to

[81] Benedict XVI, "Address to H. E. Mr. Nigel Marcus Baker, New Ambassador of the United Kingdom of Great Britain and Northern Ireland to the Holy See," Apostolic Palace, Castel Gandolfo, September 9, 2011.

> encourage the new generations in their search for and discovery of the truth about man and God. Bl. John Henry Newman's life, so strongly associated with the academic world, confirmed the importance and beauty of promoting an educational environment in which intellectual formation, ethics and religious commitment walk hand in hand.[82]

Pope Benedict XVI, following the custom of his predecessors, issued a message on January 24, 2013, for the upcoming 47th World Communications Day on May 12, 2013. In it he wrote about the cardinal for the last time during his pontificate — in fact, he had already abdicated the papacy by the time World Communications Day was celebrated. He wrote about people of faith who, due to their love and commitment to the Lord, wished to share His message. He encouraged such people to do what Blessed Newman had done, to imitate him in following the "kindly light" of faith:

> For those who have accepted the gift of faith with an open heart, the most radical response to mankind's questions about love, truth and the meaning of life — questions certainly not absent from social networks — are found in the person of Jesus Christ. It is natural for those who have faith to desire to share it, respectfully and tactfully, with those they meet in the digital forum. Ultimately, however, if our efforts to share the Gospel bring forth good fruit, it is always because of the power of the word of God itself to touch hearts, prior to any of our own efforts. Trust in the power of God's work must always be greater than any confidence we place in

[82] Benedict XVI, "Address to Participants in the World Congress for the Pastoral Care of International Students," Consistory Hall, December 2, 2011.

> human means. In the digital environment, too, where it is easy for heated and divisive voices to be raised and where sensationalism can at times prevail, we are called to attentive discernment. Let us recall in this regard that Elijah recognized the voice of God not in the great and strong wind, not in the earthquake or the fire, but in "a still, small voice" (1 Kg. 19:11–12). We need to trust in the fact that the basic human desire to love and to be loved, and to find meaning and truth—a desire which God himself has placed in the heart of every man and woman—keeps our contemporaries ever open to what Blessed Cardinal Newman called the "kindly light" of faith.[83]

Pope Francis

Cardinal Jorge Mario Bergoglio (reigned 2013–2025), a Jesuit, was born on December 17, 1936, in the district of Flores of Buenos Aires, Argentina, to an Italian couple who had emigrated to Argentina. He has a number of firsts: the first Jesuit Pope; the first Pope from the Americas and the Southern Hemisphere; the first Pope since the Syrian Pope Gregory III (reigned 731–741) in the eighth century to be born and raised outside Europe; the first Pope to choose the papal name Francis; and the first Pope to reside in Domus Sanctae Marthae guesthouse inside Vatican City.

Pope John Paul II appointed him an Auxiliary Bishop of Buenos Aires, and he was consecrated bishop on June 27, 1992. He was subsequently named Coadjutor Archbishop of Buenos Aires on June 3, 1997, becoming Metropolitan Archbishop of that see on February 28,

[83] Pope Benedict XVI, "Social Networks: Portals of Truth and Faith; New Spaces for Evangelization," Message for the 47th World Communications Day, May 12, 2013.

1998. The same sainted Pope created him a cardinal on February 21, 2001. Cardinal Bergoglio was elected Pope on March 13, 2013, on the heels of the abdication of Pope Benedict XVI on February 28, 2013.

Pope Francis's first encyclical was entitled *Lumen Fidei*, published on June 29, 2013, less than four months after his papal election. Its focus was faith. Thus, it should come as no surprise that Pope Francis made reference to Cardinal Newman. In paragraph 48, he referred to Newman's *An Essay on the Development of Christian Doctrine* (pp. 185–189):

> Since faith is one, it must be professed in all its purity and integrity. Precisely because all the articles of faith are interconnected, to deny one of them, even of those that seem least important, is tantamount to distorting the whole. Each period of history can find this or that point of faith easier or harder to accept: hence the need for vigilance in ensuring that the deposit of faith is passed on in its entirety (cf. 1 Tim. 6:20) and that all aspects of the profession of faith are duly emphasized. Indeed, inasmuch as the unity of faith is the unity of the Church, to subtract something from the faith is to subtract something from the veracity of communion. The Fathers described faith as a body, the body of truth composed of various members, by analogy with the body of Christ and its prolongation in the Church (cf. Irenaeus, *Adversus Haereses*, II, 27, 1: SC 294, 264). The integrity of the faith was also tied to the image of the Church as a virgin and her fidelity in love for Christ her spouse; harming the faith means harming communion with the Lord (cf. Augustine, *De Sancta Virginitate*, 48, 48: PL 40, 424–425: "*Servatur et in fide inviolata quaedam castitas virginalis, qua Ecclesia uni viro virgo casta coaptatur*"). The

> unity of faith, then, is the unity of a living body; this was clearly brought out by Blessed John Henry Newman when he listed among the characteristic notes for distinguishing the continuity of doctrine over time its power to assimilate everything that it meets in the various settings in which it becomes present and in the diverse cultures which it encounters (cf. *An Essay on the Development of Christian Doctrine* [Uniform Edition: Longmans, Green and Company, London, 1868–1881], 185–189), purifying all things and bringing them to their finest expression. Faith is thus shown to be universal, catholic, because its light expands in order to illumine the entire cosmos and all of history.[84]

Pope Francis published the apostolic exhortation *Evangelii Gaudium* later that same year, on November 24, 2013. It dealt with the Pope's vision of the Church as she proclaims the gospel in today's world, calling every member to an authentic personal conversion and a profound renewal within the Church herself. He quoted Cardinal Newman's preoccupation with the Christian world becoming sterile and irrelevant. He also referred to Pope Benedict XVI's call for Catholics to follow their thirst for Christ. The reference to Newman is found in paragraph 86:

> In some places a spiritual "desertification" has evidently come about, as the result of attempts by some societies to build without God or to eliminate their Christian roots. In those places "the Christian world is becoming sterile, and it is depleting itself like an overexploited ground, which transforms into a desert" (J. H. Newman, Letter of 26 January

[84] Francis, Encyclical Letter on Faith *Lumen Fidei* (June 29, 2013), no. 48.

> 1833, in *The Letters and Diaries of John Henry Newman*, vol. III, Oxford, 1979, 204). In other countries, violent opposition to Christianity forces Christians to hide their faith in their own beloved homeland. This is another painful kind of desert. But family and the workplace can also be a parched place where faith nonetheless has to be preserved and communicated. Yet "it is starting from the experience of this desert, from this void, that we can again discover the joy of believing, its vital importance for us men and women. In the desert we rediscover the value of what is essential for living; thus in today's world there are innumerable signs, often expressed implicitly or negatively, of the thirst for God, for the ultimate meaning of life. And in the desert people of faith are needed who, by the example of their own lives, point out the way to the Promised Land and keep hope alive" (Benedict XVI, Homily at Mass for the Opening of the Year of Faith [11 October 2012]: AAS 104 [2012], 881). In these situations we are called to be living sources of water from which others can drink. At times, this becomes a heavy cross, but it was from the cross, from his pierced side, that our Lord gave himself to us as a source of living water. Let us not allow ourselves to be robbed of hope![85]

Pope Francis published a new apostolic constitution entitled *Veritatis Gaudium* on December 8, 2017, which entered into force the following January 29. The document deals with Catholic universities and their faculties. In essence, it does not deal with Catholic institutions of higher education that bestow no academic degrees. He referred to Cardinal

[85] Francis, Apostolic Exhortation on the Proclamation of the Gospel in Today's World *Evangelii Gaudium* (November 24, 2013), no. 86.

Newman's idea of a well-rounded approach for university students, quoting from Newman's *The Idea of a University*: "It follows that someone trained in the framework of the institutions promoted by the system of ecclesiastical studies — as Blessed John Henry Newman wished for — ought to know "just where he and his science stand; he has come to it, as it were, from a height; he has taken a survey of all knowledge."[86]

Pope Francis canonized five Blesseds on October 13, 2019. One of them was John Henry Newman. The Holy Father referred to Newman's "kindly light," which guided him through his virtuous life — virtues which not only guide ordinary faithful Christians in personal holiness but also in relating to others.

> To cry out. To walk. To give thanks. Today we give thanks to the Lord for our new Saints. They walked by faith and now we invoke their intercession. Three of them were religious women; they show us that the consecrated life is a journey of love at the existential peripheries of the world. Saint Marguerite Bays, on the other hand, was a seamstress; she speaks to us of the power of simple prayer, enduring patience and silent self-giving. That is how the Lord made the splendor of Easter radiate in her life, in her humbleness. Such is the holiness of daily life, which Saint John Henry Newman described in these words: "The Christian has a deep, silent, hidden peace, which the world sees not.... The Christian is cheerful, easy, kind, gentle, courteous, candid, unassuming; has no pretense ... with so little that is unusual or striking in his bearing, that he may easily be taken at first sight for an ordinary man" (*Parochial and Plain Sermons*, V, 5).

[86] Apostolic Constitution on Ecclesiastical Universities and Faculties *Veritatis Gaudium* (January 29, 2018), no. 4(c).

> Let us ask to be like that, "kindly lights" amid the encircling gloom. Jesus, "stay with me, and then I shall begin to shine as Thou shinest: so to shine as to be a light to others" (*Meditations on Christian Doctrine*, VII, 3). Amen.[87]

The same Pontiff also referred to this light in his book, *My Door Is Always Open: A Conversation on Faith, Hope and the Church in a Time of Change*.[88]

Pope Francis, addressing the rectors, professors, students, and staff of the pontifical universities in Rome on February 25, 2023, described the activities within the academic setting as similar to singing in a choir. With this in mind, he referred to St. Newman in the following words:

> The university is a school of harmony and consonance among different voices and instruments. It is not a school of uniformity: no, it is one of harmony and consonance among different voices and instruments. Saint John Henry Newman describes the university as the place where different forms of knowledge and perspectives are expressed in symphony; they complement, correct, and counterbalance each other (*The Idea of a University*, 101).[89]

Finally, in his encyclical *Dilexit Nos*, Pope Francis referred to Newman's approach to dialogue with the Lord. It entails the mutual speaking of

87 Francis, "Homily at Holy Mass and Canonization of the Blesseds: John Henry Newman, Giuseppina Vannini, Mariam Thresia Chiramel Mankidiyan, Dulce Lopes Pontes, Marguerite Bays," St. Peter's Square, October 13, 2019.

88 (Bloomsbury Continuum, 2014), 118.

89 Francis, "Address to Rectors, Professors, Students and Staff of the Roman Pontifical Universities and Institutions," Paul VI Audience Hall, February 25, 2023.

the Divine and human hearts, and what takes place during this dialogue between God and a human being:

> Saint John Henry Newman took as his motto the phrase *Cor ad cor loquitur,* since, beyond all our thoughts and ideas, the Lord saves us by speaking to our hearts from his Sacred Heart. This realization led him, the distinguished intellectual, to recognize that his deepest encounter with himself and with the Lord came not from his reading or reflection, but from his prayerful dialogue, heart to heart, with Christ, alive and present. It was in the Eucharist that Newman encountered the living heart of Jesus, capable of setting us free, giving meaning to each moment of our lives, and bestowing true peace: "O most Sacred, most loving Heart of Jesus, Thou art concealed in the Holy Eucharist, and Thou beatest for us still.... I worship Thee then with all my best love and awe, with my fervent affection, with my most subdued, most resolved will. O my God, when Thou dost condescend to suffer me to receive Thee, to eat and drink Thee, and Thou for a while takest up Thy abode within me, O make my heart beat with Thy Heart. Purify it of all that is earthly, all that is proud and sensual, all that is hard and cruel, of all perversity, of all disorder, of all deadness. So fill it with Thee, that neither the events of the day nor the circumstances of the time may have power to ruffle it, but that in Thy love and Thy fear it may have peace" (Saint John Henry Newman, *Meditations and Devotions,* London, 1912, Part III [XVI], par. 3, pp. 573–574).[90]

[90] Francis, Encyclical Letter on the Human and Divine Love of the Heart of Jesus Christ *Dilexit Nos* (October 24, 2024), no. 26.

Thus, with the exceptions of two Popes, Benedict XV (1914–1922) and Blessed John Paul I (1978), every reigning Pope of the last century and a half has spoken of Cardinal Newman. It is entirely understandable why these two Popes were silent on the saint: Benedict XV was busy with World War I and its aftermath, while John Paul I's extremely short papacy of thirty-three days did not provide him with any occasion to speak of the sainted cardinal.

FOUR

Other Entities and Cardinal Newman

It has been indicated elsewhere that St. John Henry Newman was perceived as a precursor of the Second Vatican Council. A number of Council documents make direct and indirect reference to his writings.

Pope Paul VI promulgated the Council's Dogmatic Constitution on Divine Revelation, *Dei Verbum,* on November 18, 1965. It was one of the major documents of the Council. Paragraph 8 of this document carried in its background what was taught by Cardinal Newman as a person of faith, great scholar, and teacher, though it did not identify him by name.

> 8. And so the apostolic preaching, which is expressed in a special way in the inspired books, was to be preserved by an unending succession of preachers until the end of time. Therefore, the Apostles, handing on what they themselves had received, warn the faithful to hold fast to the traditions which they have learned either by word of mouth or by letter (see Thessalonians 2:15), and to fight in defense of the faith handed on once and for all (see Jude 1:3; cf. Second Council of Nicaea: Denzinger 303: 602); Fourth Council of Constance, session X, canon 1,

ibid. 336: 650–652). Now what was handed on by the Apostles includes everything which contributes toward the holiness of life and increase in faith of the peoples of God; and so the Church, in her teaching, life and worship, perpetuates and hands on to all generations all that she herself is, all that she believes.

This tradition which comes from the Apostles develops in the Church with the help of the Holy Spirit (Second Council of Orange, canon 7, ibid. 180: 377; First Vatican Council, Dogmatic Constitution on the Church, chapter 3, "On Faith", ibid. 1791: 3010). For there is a growth in the understanding of the realities and the words which have been handed down. This happens through the contemplation and study made by believers, who treasure these things in their hearts (Luke 2:19, 51) through a penetrating understanding of the spiritual realities which they experience, and through the preaching of those who have received through Episcopal succession the sure gift of truth. For as the centuries succeed one another, the Church constantly moves forward toward the fullness of divine truth until the words of God reach their complete fulfillment in her.

The words of the Holy Fathers witness to the presence of this living tradition, whose wealth is poured into the practice and life of the believing and praying Church. Through the same tradition the Church's full canon of the sacred books is known, and the sacred writings themselves are more profoundly understood and unceasingly made active in her; and thus God, who spoke of old, uninterruptedly converses with the bride of His beloved Son; and the Holy Spirit, through whom the living voice of the Gospel resounds in the Church, and through her, in the world,

> leads unto all truth those who believe and makes the word of Christ dwell abundantly in them (cf. Col. 3:16).[91]

The same Pope promulgated the Dogmatic Constitution *Lumen Gentium* on November 21, 1964. Newman's ecclesiology anticipated the teaching in *Lumen Gentium.* He was a lonely pioneer when he wrote the article entitled "On Consulting the Faithful in Matters of Doctrine." The rediscovery of the charismatic dimension of the Church in the first two chapters of *Lumen Gentium* echoes Newman's teaching, both as an Anglican and as a Catholic, on the importance of laity belonging to Church movements and communities, which would emerge in such abundance after the Council. Paragraph 12 states:

> The holy people of God shares also in Christ's prophetic office; it spreads abroad a living witness to Him, especially by means of a life of faith and charity and by offering God a sacrifice of praise, the tribute of lips which give praise to His name (cf. Heb. 13:15). The entire body of the faithful, anointed as they are by the Holy One (cf. Jn. 2:20, 27), cannot err in matters of belief. They manifest this special property by means of the whole peoples' supernatural discernment in matters of faith when "from the Bishops down to the last of the lay faithful" they show universal agreement in matters of faith and morals. The discernment in matters of faith is aroused and sustained by the Spirit of truth. It is exercised under the guidance of the sacred teaching authority, in faithful and respectful obedience to which the people of God accepts that which is not just the word of men but truly the

[91] Vatican Council II, Dogmatic Constitution on Divine Revelation *Dei Verbum* (November 18, 1965), no. 8.

> word of God (cf. 1 Thess. 2:13). Through it, the people of God adheres unwaveringly to the faith given once and for all to the saints (cf. Jud. 3), penetrates it more deeply with right thinking, and applies it more fully in its life.
>
> It is not only through the sacraments and the ministries of the Church that the Holy Spirit sanctifies and leads the people of God and enriches it with virtues, but, "allotting his gifts to everyone according as He wills ["](1 Cor. 12:11), He distributes special graces among the faithful of every rank. By these gifts He makes them fit and ready to undertake the various tasks and offices which contribute toward the renewal and building up of the Church, according to the words of the Apostle: "The manifestation of the Spirit is given to everyone for profit" (cf. 1 Thess. 5:12, 19–21). These charisms, whether they be more outstanding or the more simple and widely diffused, are to be received with thanksgiving and consolation for they are perfectly suited to and useful for the needs of the Church. Extraordinary gifts are not to be sought after, nor are the fruits of apostolic labor to be presumptuously expected from their use; but judgment as to their genuinity and proper use belongs to those who are appointed leaders in the Church, to those whose special competence it belongs, not indeed to extinguish the Spirit, but to test all things and hold fast to that which is good (cf. Jn. 11:52).[92]

The Holy See has a number of important entities which, until recently, carried the designation *congregation*. They are now called *dicasteries*.

[92] Vatican Council II, Dogmatic Constitution on the Church *Lumen Gentium* (November 21, 1964), no. 12.

One of them is the Dicastery for the Doctrine of the Faith. This eminent department issued a document on February 2, 2013, called "The Call to Communion: *Anglicanorum coetibus* and Ecclesial Unity."[93] The document was a major address delivered by Archbishop (later Cardinal) Gerhard Ludwig Müller at a symposium in Houston, Texas, on the Ordinariate of the Chair of St. Peter. This personal ordinariate was established by Pope Benedict XVI on November 4, 2009, to receive former Anglican priests into the Catholic Church, where they may continue with their ministry, now as Catholic priests, whether they are married or not. Müller referred to Cardinal Newman when he stated the following:

> Building this culture of communion begins with advancing a narrative to explain to Catholics and non-Catholics alike the abiding value of unity, the integrity of the faith, and loyalty to the Holy Father and to the Church's Magisterium. In other words, you must propose ever anew the raison d'être of the Ordinariate or, in the words of St. Peter himself, "Always be prepared to give to anyone who asks a reason for the hope that is in you" (1 Pt. 3:15). Sadly, many people see the world through the polarized lens of division and political factions, and so numerous articles have appeared about *Anglicanorum coetibus* which describe the Holy Father as an ecumenical poacher and characterize those who seek communion as disgruntled reactionaries. It falls to us as architects of communion to provide the correct interpretation of the Ordinariate as the fruit of a trajectory towards unity which began over 150 years ago in the Oxford Movement through

93 The document refers to Benedict XVI, Apostolic Constitution Providing for Personal Ordinariates for Anglicans Entering into Full Communion with the Catholic Church *Anglicanorum Coetibus* (November 4, 2009).

> great figures like Blessed John Henry Newman. The right narrative about the great adventure of fidelity and about the Ordinariate as an eloquent expression of ecumenism is too important to leave to others to write for us.[94]

The same congregation, still under the same Prefect, now a cardinal, issued a letter on May 15, 2015, entitled *Iuvenescit Ecclesia*. It was addressed to the Bishops of the Universal Catholic Church regarding the relationship between hierarchical and charismatic gifts in the life and mission of the Church. It dealt with the development of charisms in Church doctrine, and it quoted Cardinal Newman's *Sermons Bearing on Subjects of the Day* in paragraph 13:

> The charismatic gifts given to individuals actually belong to the Church herself and are ordered towards a more intense ecclesial life. This perspective is present also in the writings of Blessed John Henry Newman: "Thus the heart of every Christian ought to represent in miniature the Catholic Church, since one Spirit makes both the whole Church and every member of it to be His Temple" (J. H. Newman, *Sermons Bearing on Subjects of the Day*, London 1869, 132). Thus, the falseness of any contradiction between or mere juxtaposition of the hierarchical and charismatic gifts is rendered more evident.[95]

94 Gerhard Ludwig Müller, "The Call to Communion: *Anglicanorum coetibus* and Ecclesial Unity," Symposium on the Ordinariate of the Chair of St. Peter, St. Mary's Seminary, Houston, Texas, February 2, 2013, https://press.vatican.va/roman_curia/congregations/cfaith/muller/rc_con_cfaith_doc_20130202_anglicanorum-coetibus_en.html.

95 Congregation for the Doctrine of the Faith, *Letter "Iuvenescit Ecclesia" to the Bishops of the Catholic Church Regarding the Relationship Between Hierarchical and Charismatic Gifts in the Life and the Mission of the Church* (May 15, 2016), no. 13.

The Pope alone establishes in the Vatican what are called *commissions*, and he assigns to each a specific purpose and role. The task of the International Theological Commission is to help the Holy See, and primarily the Dicastery for the Doctrine of the Faith, in examining doctrinal questions of major importance. The Commission issued a lengthy statement on November 29, 2011, entitled *Theology Today: Perspective, Principles and Criteria*. It quoted Newman's *The Via Media of the Anglican Church* in its paragraph 42, when speaking about the relationship between bishops and theologians.

> The relationship between bishops and theologians is often good and trusting on both sides, with due respect for one another's callings and responsibilities. For example, bishops attend and participate in national and regional gatherings of theological associations, call on theological experts as they formulate their own teaching and policies, and visit and support theological faculties and schools in their dioceses. Inevitably, there will be tensions at times in the relationship between theologians and bishops. In his profound analysis of the dynamic interaction, within the living organism of the Church, of the three offices of Christ as prophet, priest and king, Blessed John Henry Newman acknowledged the possibility of such "chronic collisions or contrasts," and it is well to remember that he saw them as "lying in the nature of the case" (John Henry Newman, "Preface to the Third Edition," in *The Via Media of the Anglican Church*, ed. H. D. Wiedner [Oxford: Clarendon Press, 1990], pp. 10–57). "Theology is the fundamental and regulating principle of the whole Church system," he wrote, and yet "theology cannot always have

> its own way" (Newman, "Preface to the Third Edition," pp. 29–30).[96]

The same Commission, on July 8, 2014, issued another document, entitled *Sensus Fidei in the Life of the Church*. It made extensive references to, and at times quoted, Cardinal Newman's writings on the subject. It quoted Newman's *On Consulting the Faithful in Matters of Doctrine* and *The Arians of the Fourth Century*. These quotes and references are found in paragraphs 26, 27, 36, 37, 38, 39, 43, 46, and 77.[97] They confirm the great influence Newman has, even in our own time.

> 26. In the first five centuries, the faith of the Church as a whole proved decisive in determining the canon of Scripture and in defining major doctrines concerning, for example, the divinity of Christ, the perpetual virginity and divine motherhood of Mary, and the veneration and invocation of the saints. In some cases, as Blessed John Henry Newman (1801–90) remarked, the faith of the laity, in particular, played a crucial role. The most striking example was in the famous controversy in the fourth century with the Arians, who were condemned at the Council of Nicaea (325 AD), where the divinity of Jesus Christ was defined. From then until the Council of Constantinople (381 AD), however, there continued to be uncertainty among the bishops. During that period, "the divine tradition

[96] International Theological Commission, *Theology Today: Perspectives, Principles and Criteria* (March 8, 2012), no. 42, https://www.vatican.va/roman_curia/congregations/cfaith/cti_documents/rc_cti_doc_20111129_teologia-oggi_en.html.

[97] International Theological Commission, *Sensus Fidei in the Life of the Church* (July 8, 2014), https://www.vatican.va/roman_curia/congregations/cfaith/cti_documents/rc_cti_20140610_sensus-fidei_en.html.

committed to the infallible Church was proclaimed and maintained far more by the faithful than by the Episcopate." "[T]here was a temporary suspense of the functions of the '*Ecclesia docens*.' The body of Bishops failed in their confession of the faith. They spoke variously, one against another; there was nothing, after Nicaea, of firm, unvarying, consistent testimony, for nearly sixty years."[98]

27. Newman also commented that "in a later age, when the learned Benedictines of Germany and France were perplexed in their enunciation of the doctrine of the Real Presence, Paschasius (c.790–c.860) was supported by the faithful in his maintenance of it" (Newman, *On Consulting the Faithful*, 104). Something similar happened with respect to the dogma, defined by Pope Benedict XII in the constitution, *Benedictus Deus* (1336), regarding the beatific vision, enjoyed already by souls after purgatory and before the day of judgement: "the tradition, on which the definition was made, was manifested in the *consensus fidelium*, with a luminousness which the succession of Bishops, though many of them were '*Sancti Patres ab ipsis Apostolorum temporibus*,' did not furnish." "Most considerable deference was paid to the 'sensus fidelium'; their opinion and advice indeed was not asked, but their testimony was

[98] In the original document, there is a footnote here, containing the following: John Henry Newman, *On Consulting the Faithful in Matters of Doctrine*, edited with an introduction by John Coulson (London: Geoffrey Chapman, 1961), pp. 75–101; at 75 and 77. See also his *The Arians of the Fourth Century* (1833; 3rd ed. 1871). Congar expresses some caution with regard to the use of Newman's analysis of this matter; see, Congar, *Jalons pour une Théologie du Laïcat*, p. 395; [English translation]: *Lay People in the Church*, pp. 285–6).

taken, their feelings consulted, their impatience, I had almost said, feared (Newman, *On Consulting the Faithful*, 70). The continuing development, among the faithful, of belief in, and devotion to, the Immaculate Conception of the Blessed Virgin Mary, in spite of opposition to the doctrine by certain theologians, is another major example of the role played in the Middle Ages by the *sensus fidelium*.

36. John Henry Newman initially investigated the *sensus fidei fidelium* to resolve his difficulty concerning the development of doctrine. He was the first to publish an entire treatise on the latter topic, *An Essay on the Development of Christian Doctrine* (1845), and to spell out the characteristics of faithful development. To distinguish between true and false developments, he adopted Augustine's norm — the general consent of the whole Church, "*Securus judicat orbis terrarum*" — but he saw that an infallible authority is necessary to maintain the Church in the truth.

37. Using insights from Möhler and Newman (In 1847, Newman met Perrone and they discussed Newman's ideas about the development of doctrine. Newman used the notion of the *sensus ecclesiae* in this context. Cf. T. Lynch, ed., "The Newman-Perrone Paper on Development," *Gregorianum* 16 (1935), pp.402–447, esp. ch. 3, nn. 2, 5.), Perrone retrieved the patristic understanding of the *sensus fidelium* in order to respond to a widespread desire for a papal definition of Mary's Immaculate Conception; he found in the unanimous consent, or *conspiratio*, of the faithful and their pastors a warrant for the apostolic origin of this doctrine. He maintained that the most distinguished theologians attributed

probative force to the *sensus fidelium*, and that the strength of one "instrument of tradition" can make up for the deficit of another, e.g., "the silence of the Fathers" (Ioannis Perrone, *De Immaculato B. V. Mariae Conceptu an Dogmatico Decreto definiri possit* [Romae, 1847], 139, 143–145).

38. The influence of Perrone's research on Pope Pius IX's decision to proceed with the definition of the Immaculate Conception is evident from the fact that before he defined it the Pope asked the bishops of the world to report to him in writing regarding the devotion of their clergy and faithful people to the conception of the Immaculate Virgin (See Pope Pius IX, Encyclical Letter, *Ubi primum* (1849), n.6). In the apostolic constitution containing the definition, *Ineffabilis Deus* (1854), Pope Pius IX said that although he already knew the mind of the bishops on this matter, he had particularly asked the bishops to inform him of the piety and devotion of their faithful in this regard, and he concluded that "Holy Scripture, venerable Tradition, the constant mind of the Church [*perpetuus Ecclesiae sensus*], the remarkable agreement of Catholic bishops and the faithful [*singularis catholicorum Antistitum ac fidelium conspiratio*], and the memorable Acts and Constitutions of our predecessors" all wonderfully illustrated and proclaimed the doctrine (Pope Pius IX, Apostolic Constitution, *Ineffabilis Deus* [1854]). He thus used the language of Perrone's treatise to describe the combined testimony of the bishops and the faithful. Newman highlighted the word, *conspiratio*, and commented: "the two, the Church teaching and the Church taught, are put together, as one twofold testimony,

illustrating each other, and never to be divided" (Newman, *On Consulting the Faithful*, pp. 70-71).

39. When Newman later wrote *On Consulting the Faithful in Matters of Doctrine* (1859), it was to demonstrate that the faithful (as distinct from their pastors) have their own, active role to play in conserving and transmitting the faith. "The tradition of the Apostles" is "committed to the whole Church in its various constituents and functions *per modum unius*," but the bishops and the lay faithful bear witness to it in diverse ways. The tradition, he says, "manifests itself variously at various times: sometimes by the mouth of the episcopacy, sometimes by the doctors, sometimes by the people, sometimes by liturgies, rites, ceremonies, and customs, by events, disputes, movements, and all those other phenomena which are comprised under the name of history." (Newman, *On Consulting the Faithful*, p.63, cf. p.65. Newman usually distinguishes the "pastors" and the "faithful." Sometimes he adds the "doctors" (theologians) as a distinct class of witnesses, and he includes the lower clergy among the "faithful" unless he specifies the "lay faithful.") For Newman, "there is something in the '*pastorum et fidelium conspiratio*' which is not in the pastors alone" (Newman, *On Consulting the Faithful*, 104). In this work, Newman quoted at length from the arguments proposed over a decade earlier by Giovanni Perrone in favor of the definition of the Immaculate Conception (Newman, *On Consulting the Faithful*, 64–70; cf. above, no. 37).

43. Yves M.J. Congar (1904–1995) contributed significantly to the development of the doctrine of the *sensus fidei*

fidelis and the *sensus fidei fidelium*.... Congar was acquainted with Newman's work and adopted the same scheme (i.e. the threefold office of the Church, and the *sensus fidelium* as an expression of the prophetic office) without, however, tracing it directly to Newman (See Congar, *Jalons pour une Théologie du Laïcat,* chapter 6. The scheme is found in the Preface of the third edition of Newman's *Via Media* [1877]).

46. The *sensus fidei* is also evoked in the council's teaching on the development of doctrine, in the context of the transmission of the apostolic faith. *Dei Verbum* says that the apostolic Tradition "makes progress in the Church, with the help of the Holy Spirit." "There is a growth in insight into the realities and words that are being passed on," and the council identifies three ways in which this happens: "through the contemplation and study of believers who ponder these things in their hearts"; "from the intimate sense of spiritual realities which they experience (*ex intima spiritualium rerum quam experiuntur intelligentia*)"; and "from the preaching of those [the bishops] who have received ... the sure charism of truth" (*Dei Verbum,* no. 8). Although this passage does not name the *sensus fidei,* the contemplation, study, and experience of believers to which it refers are all clearly associated with the *sensus fidei,* and most commentators agree that the Council Fathers were consciously invoking Newman's theory of the development of doctrine. When this text is read in light of the description of the *sensus fidei* in *Lumen Gentium* 12 as a supernatural appreciation of the faith, aroused by the Holy Spirit, by which people guided by their pastors adhere unfailingly to

> the faith, it is readily seen to express the same idea. When referring to "the remarkable harmony" that should exist between the bishops and the faithful in the practice and profession of the faith handed on by the apostles, *Dei Verbum* actually uses the very expression found in the definitions of both Marian dogmas, "*singularis fiat Antistitum et fidelium conspiratio*" (*Dei Verbum*, no. 10; cf. *Ineffabilis Deus*, no.18, and *Munificentissimus Deus*, no.12).
>
> 77. The magisterium also judges with authority whether opinions which are present among the people of God, and which may seem to be the *sensus fidelium*, actually correspond to the truth of the Tradition received from the Apostles. As Newman said: "the gift of discerning, discriminating, defining, promulgating, and enforcing any portion of that tradition resides solely in the *Ecclesia docens*" (Newman, *On Consulting the Faithful*, 63). Thus, judgement regarding the authenticity of the *sensus fidelium* belongs ultimately not to the faithful themselves nor to theology but to the magisterium. Nevertheless, as already emphasized, the faith which it serves is the faith of the Church, which lives in all of the faithful, so it is always within the communion life of the Church that the magisterium exercises its essential ministry of oversight.

The same Commission published another article, entitled *Synodality in the Life and Mission of the Church*, on March 2, 2018. It makes reference to Cardinal Newman's advocacy of the role of the faithful in paragraph 38:

> The need for a pertinent and consistent re-launch of Synodal practice in the Catholic Church became clear as early as the nineteenth century, thanks to prophetic writers like Johann Adam Möhler (1796–1838), Antonio Rosmini (1797–1855) and John Henry Newman (1801–1890), who returned to the normative sources of Scripture and Tradition, heralding the providential renewal that came with the biblical, liturgical and patristic movements. They stressed that a primary and fundamental element in the life of the Church is the dimension of communion, which implies an ordered synodal practice on every level, giving due importance to the *sensus fidei fidelium*, intrinsically related to the specific ministry of the Bishops and the Pope. The emergence of a new climate in ecumenical relationships with other Churches and ecclesial communities, and a more careful discernment of the advanced demands of modern consciousness concerning the participation of every citizen in running society, call for a new and deeper experience and presentation of the mystery of the Church as intrinsically synodal.[99]

John Henry Newman reflected throughout his life on the nature of Divine Revelation and biblical inspiration, and the role of Tradition in the composition and interpretation of Sacred Scripture. His teaching influenced a number of theologians who participated in the Second Vatican Council as theological experts (*periti*), like the two Dominicans Yves-Marie Congar and Edward Schillebeeckx, and the Jesuit Henri

[99] International Theological Commission, *Synodality in the Life and Mission of the Church* (March 2, 2018), https://www.vatican.va/roman_curia/congregations/cfaith/cti_documents/rc_cti_20180302_sinodalita_en.html.

de Lubac. The English Bishop Christopher Butler, O.S.B., himself a convert from Anglicanism, stated that

> Newman's theology was based almost uniquely on the Bible. Its real foundations emerge in the *Parochial and Plain Sermons* and the *University Sermons* of his Oxford days, which embody a dialectical progress [from the] rather narrow biblicism of traditional Protestantism to that evolutionary vision which comes to light in the last *University Sermon*, on the "Principle of Development."[100]

The previous chapter presented extensive quotes from Pope Benedict XVI. However, there is also important material dating to the period before his papal election. It is no secret that Joseph Ratzinger was a great admirer of Cardinal Newman, and this endured throughout his life as a seminarian, priest, archbishop, cardinal, and Pope. In his capacity as the Prefect of the Congregation for the Doctrine of the Faith, Cardinal Ratzinger delivered a lecture in Rome on April 28, 1990, to mark the first centenary of the death of Cardinal Newman. In his humble way, Cardinal Ratzinger recounted how he had related to Cardinal Newman since his years as a seminarian. He emphasized Newman's eminent teaching of conscience and how Newman's obedience to his own conscience led him to convert to the Roman Catholic Faith.

> I do not feel competent to speak on Newman's figure or work, but perhaps it is meaningful if I tell a little about my own way to Newman, in which indeed something is

[100] Bishop Christopher Butler, O.S.B., delivered this paper, "Newman and the Second Vatican Council," at The Rediscovery of Newman: An Oxford Symposium. The text can be found at Vatican II — The Voice of the Church, https://www.vatican2voice.org/3butlerwrites/newman.htm.

reflected of the presence of this great English theologian in the intellectual and spiritual struggle of our time.

In January 1946, when I began my study of theology in the Seminary in Freising, . . . an older student was assigned as prefect to our group, who had begun to work on a dissertation on Newman's theology of conscience even before the beginning of the war. In all the years of his military service he had not lost sight of this theme, which he now turned to with new enthusiasm and energy.

We were soon bonded by a personal friendship, wholly centered on the great problems of philosophy and theology. Of course, Newman was always present. . . . For us at that time, Newman's teaching on conscience became an important foundation for theological personalism, which was drawing us all in its sway. Our image of the human being as well as our image of the Church was permeated by this point of departure . . . it was liberating and essential for us to know that the "we" of the Church does not rest on a cancellation of conscience, but that, exactly the opposite, it can only develop from conscience.

Precisely because Newman interpreted the existence of the human being from conscience, that is, from the relationship between God and the soul, was it clear that this personalism is not individualism, and that being bound by conscience does not mean being free to make random choices — the exact opposite is the case.

It was from Newman that we learned to understand the primacy of the Pope. Freedom of conscience, Newman told us, is not identical with the right "to dispense with conscience, to ignore a Lawgiver and Judge, to be independent of unseen obligations."

Thus, conscience in its true sense is the bedrock of Papal authority; its power comes from revelation that completes natural conscience, which is imperfectly enlightened, and "the championship of the Moral Law and of conscience is its raison d'être."... This teaching on conscience has become ever more important for me in the continued development of the Church and the world.

Newman had become a convert as a man of conscience; it was his conscience that led him out of the old ties and securities into the world of Catholicism, which was difficult and strange for him. But this way of conscience is everything except a way of self-sufficient subjectivity: it is a way of obedience to objective truth.

The second step in Newman's lifelong journey of conversion was overcoming the subjective evangelical position in favor of an understanding of Christendom based on the objectivity of dogma. In this connection I find a formulation from one of his early sermons to be especially significant today:

"True Christendom is shown ... in obedience and not through a state of consciousness. Thus, the whole duty and work of a Christian is made up of these two parts, Faith and Obedience; 'looking unto Jesus' (Heb. 2: 9) ... and acting according to His will.... I conceive that we are in danger, in this day, of insisting on neither of these as we ought; regarding all true and careful consideration of the Object of faith as barren orthodoxy, technical subtlety ... and ... making the test of our being religious to consist in our having what is called a spiritual state of heart...."

In this context some sentences from *The Arians of the Fourth Century*, which may sound rather astonishing at first, seem important to me: "… to detect and to approve the principle on which … peace is grounded in Scripture; to submit to the dictation of truth, as such, as a primary authority in matters of political and private conduct; to understand … zeal to be prior in the succession of Christian graces to benevolence."

For me it is always fascinating to see and consider how in just this way and only in this way, through commitment to the truth, to God, conscience receives its rank, dignity and strength. …

Newman's teaching on the development of doctrine … I regard along with his doctrine on conscience as his decisive contribution to the renewal of theology. …

At this point I would only like to refer again to the biographical background of this concept. It is known how Newman's insight into the ideas of development influenced his way to Catholicism. But it is not just a matter of an unfolding of ideas. In the concept of development, Newman's own life plays a role. That seems to become visible to me in his well-known words: "… to live is to change, and to be perfect is to have changed often."

Throughout his entire life, Newman was a person converting, a person being transformed, and thus he always remained and became ever more himself.

Here the figure of St Augustine comes to my mind, with whom Newman was so associated. When Augustine was converted in the garden at Cassiciacum he understood conversion according to the system of the revered master Plotin and the Neo-Platonic philosophers. He thought that his past sinful life would now be definitively cast off; from now on the convert would be someone wholly new and

> different, and his further journey would be a steady climb to the ever purer heights of closeness to God....
>
> In the idea of "development" Newman had written his own experience of a never finished conversion and interpreted for us, not only the way of Christian doctrine, but that of the Christian life.
>
> The characteristic of the great Doctor of the Church, it seems to me, is that he teaches not only through his thought and speech but also by his life, because within him, thought and life are interpenetrated and defined. If this is so, then Newman belongs to the great teachers of the Church, because he both touches our hearts and enlightens our thinking.[101]

In February 1991, Cardinal Ratzinger delivered a presentation on "Conscience and Truth," during the Tenth Workshop for Bishops in Dallas, Texas. He elaborated on what he had stated during his lecture in Rome, again linking Newman to St. Augustine, but now adding St. Thomas More. He again spoke about the primary role of conscience in seeking truth.

> A first glance should be directed to Cardinal Newman, whose life and work could be designated a single great commentary on the question of conscience.... I would simply like to try to indicate the place of conscience in the whole of Newman's life and thought. The insights gained from this will hopefully sharpen our view of present problems

[101] Cardinal Joseph Ratzinger, "Presentation on the Occasion of the First Centenary of the Death of Card. John Henry Newman," Rome, April 28, 1990, https://www.vatican.va/roman_curia/congregations/cfaith/documents/rc_con_cfaith_doc_19900428_ratzinger-newman_en.html.

and establish the link to history, that is, both to the great witnesses of conscience and to the origin of the Christian doctrine of living according to conscience. When the subject of Newman and conscience is raised, the famous sentence from his letter to the Duke of Norfolk immediately comes to mind: "Certainly, if I am obliged to bring religion into after-dinner toasts, (which indeed does not seem quite the thing), I shall drink — to the Pope, if you please, — still to conscience first and to the Pope afterwards." In contrast to the statements of Gladstone, Newman sought to make a clear avowal of the papacy. And in contrast to mistaken forms of ultra-Montanism, Newman embraced an interpretation of the papacy which is only then correctly conceived when it is viewed together with the primacy of conscience, a papacy not put in opposition to the primacy of conscience but based on it and guaranteeing it. Modern man, who presupposes the opposition of authority to subjectivity, has difficulty understanding this. For him, conscience stands on the side of subjectivity and is the expression of the freedom of the subject. Authority, on the other hand, appears to him as the constraint on, threat to, and even the negation of, freedom. So then, we must go deeper to recover a vision in which this kind of opposition does not obtain.

For Newman, the middle term which establishes the connection between authority and subjectivity is truth. I do not hesitate to say that truth is the central thought of Newman's intellectual grappling. Conscience is central for him because truth stands in the middle. To put it differently, the centrality of the concept conscience, for Newman, is linked to the prior centrality of the concept truth, and can only be understood from this vantage point. The dominance of the idea of conscience in Newman does not signify that he, in the nineteenth century and in contrast to "objectivistic" neo-scholasticism, espoused a philosophy or theology of subjectivity. Certainly, the subject finds in Newman an attention which it had not received in Catholic theology perhaps since Saint Augustine. But it is an attention in the line of Augustine and not in that of the subjectivist philosophy of the modern age. On the occasion of his elevation to Cardinal, Newman declared that most of his life was a struggle against the spirit of liberalism in religion. We might add, also against Christian subjectivism, as he found it in the Evangelical movement of his time and which admittedly had provided him the first step on his lifelong road to conversion. Conscience for Newman does not mean that the subject is the standard vis-a-vis the claims of authority in a truthless world, a world which lives from the compromise between the claims of the subject and the claims of the social order. Much more than that, conscience signifies the perceptible and demanding presence of the voice of truth in the subject himself. It is the overcoming of mere subjectivity in the encounter of the interiority of man with the truth from God. The verse Newman composed in 1833 in Sicily is characteristic: "I loved to choose and see my path but now, lead thou me on!" Newman's conversion to Catholicism was not for him a matter of personal taste or of subjective, spiritual need. He expressed himself on this even in 1844, on the threshold, so to speak, of his conversion: "No one can have a more unfavorable view than I of the present state of Roman Catholics." Newman was much more taken by the necessity to obey recognized truth than his own preferences, that is to say, even against his own sensitivity and bonds of friendship and ties due to similar backgrounds. It seems to me characteristic of Newman that he emphasized truth's priority over goodness in the order of virtues. Or, to put it in a way which is more understandable for us, he emphasized truth's priority over consensus, over the accommodation of groups. I would say, when we are speaking of a man of conscience, we mean one who looks at things this way. A man of conscience is one who never acquires tolerance, well-being, success, public standing, and approval on the part of prevailing opinion, at the expense of truth. In this regard, Newman is related to Britain's other great witness of conscience, Thomas More, for whom conscience was not at all an expression of subjective stubbornness or obstinate heroism. He numbered himself, in fact, among those fainthearted martyrs who only after faltering and much questioning succeed in mustering up obedience to conscience, mustering up obedience to the truth which must stand higher than any human tribunal or any type of personal taste. Thus two standards become apparent for ascertaining the presence of a real voice or conscience. First, conscience is not identical to personal wishes and taste. Secondly, conscience cannot be reduced to social advantage, to group consensus, or to the demands of political and social power.[102]

[102] Joseph Cardinal Ratzinger, "Conscience and Truth," presentation at the Tenth Workshop for Bishops, Dallas, Texas, February 1991, EWTN, https://www.ewtn.com/catholicism/library/conscience-and-truth-2468. The punctuation in this excerpt has been adapted for better readability. See also Peter Jennings, ed., *Benedict XVI and Cardinal Newman* (Family Publications, 2005), 41–52.

FIVE

Cardinal Newman, Author of Eminent Doctrine

The reason so many Catholic and non-Catholic hierarchs, institutions, and individuals have petitioned Pope Francis to declare St. John Henry Newman a Doctor of the Universal Church is his profound teachings, particularly in theology, which is perennial. In this chapter, we will survey some of the theological topics into which Newman offered important insights.

Development of Doctrine

One of Newman's major contributions is his *Essay on the Development of Christian Doctrine*. In this work, he exhibited an extraordinarily vast knowledge and understanding of Sacred Scripture; of the teachings of the early Ecumenical Councils and the heretical doctrines which they addressed, in particular Arianism; of the doctrines of and differences between the Roman Catholic Church and, especially, the Anglican Church; of the later Catholic Ecumenical Councils in Church history; and of diverse theories about this subject matter which were put forward by some of his own contemporaries.

The fundamental question about development of Christian Doctrine is as follows: Is Christianity a distinct teaching given by Jesus to His disciples — who, in turn, handed it down to their successors — that was never intended to be developed, or is it a fact that there is a historical Christianity? The first position ends up seeing doctrine as the private judgment of each individual, who interprets Sacred Scripture and other sources as he or she deems fit. On the other hand, the second position advocates the existence of a historical Christianity, which is identified with the Apostolic Church, with the early Ecumenical Councils, and, for some, with the Church of Rome. Newman's insights developed and deepened as he studied and reflected on this fundamental question — activities that eventually led him to cross the Tiber, abandon his adherence to Anglicanism, and join the Catholic Church.

Newman was not the only person who tackled this question. Some Anglican clergy who were members of the Oxford Movement also addressed it. They appealed to the dictum of the fifth-century Gallic monk, St. Vincent of Lérins, as stated in his *commonitorium*: "in the Catholic Church itself ... we hold that faith which has been believed everywhere, always, and by all."[103] St. Vincent of Lérins began the treatment of this subject by asking a question:

> Is there to be no development of religion in the Church of Christ? Certainly, there is to be development and on the largest scale.
>
> Who can be so grudging to men, so full of hate for God, as to try to prevent it? But it must truly be development of the faith, not alteration of the faith. Development means that each thing expands to be itself, while alteration means that a thing is changed from one thing into another.

[103] Vincent of Lérins, "The Commonitory of Vincent of Lérins," trans. Charles A. Heurtley, in *Sulpitius Severus, Vincent of Lérins, John Cassian: A Select Library of the Nicene and Post-Nicene Fathers of the Church*, vol. 11, eds. Philip Schaffer and Henry Wace (Christian Literature Company, 1894), 132.

The understanding, knowledge and wisdom of one and all, of individuals as well as of the whole Church, ought then to make great and vigorous progress with the passing of the ages and the centuries, but only along its own line of development, that is, with the same doctrine, the same meaning and the same import.

The religion of souls should follow the law of development of bodies. Though bodies develop and unfold their component parts with the passing of the years, they always remain what they were. There is a great difference between the flower of childhood and the maturity of age, but those who become old are the very same people who were once young. Though the condition and appearance of one and the same individual may change, it is one and the same nature, one and the same person.

The tiny members of unweaned children and the grown members of young men are still the same members. Men have the same number of limbs as children. Whatever develops at a later age was already present in seminal form; there is nothing new in old age that was not already latent in childhood.

There is no doubt, then, that the legitimate and correct rule of development, the established and wonderful order of growth, is this: in older people the fullness of years always brings to completion those members and forms that the wisdom of the Creator fashioned beforehand in their earlier years.

If, however, the human form was to turn into some shape that did not belong to its own nature, or even if something were added to the sum of its members or subtracted from it, the whole body would necessarily perish or become grotesque or at least be enfeebled. In the same way, the doctrine of the Christian religion should properly

> follow these laws of development, that is, by becoming firmer over the years, more ample in the course of time, more exalted as it advances in age.
>
> In ancient times our ancestors sowed the good seed in the harvest field of the Church. It would be very wrong and unfitting if we, their descendants, were to reap, not the genuine wheat of truth but the intrusive growth of error.
>
> On the contrary, what is right and fitting is this: there should be no inconsistency between first and last, but we should reap true doctrine from the growth of true teaching, so that when, in the course of time, those first sowings yield an increase, it may flourish and be tended in our day also.[104]

Newman agreed in principle with the above commentary, but then noted that the existential situation in the Church of the fifth century was different than the one of his time. He claimed that Anglican theologians were arbitrary in their application, because they applied Lérins's teaching to some doctrinal issues when it suited them, while they did not apply it to doctrines they rejected. He charged such theologians with anti-Catholic prejudice.

Newman proceeded to offer another kind of regulation to distinguish between authentic doctrine and its corruption in *An Essay on the Development of Christian Doctrine*. Fundamentally, Newman came to realize that ideas and doctrines were "living" and should not be considered purely intellectual beliefs or mere moral rules; instead, they should vitalize the hearts of Christians and the body of the Church, following the example of Christ. The Church, he wrote,

[104] "Commonitory of St. Vincent of Lérins" (Cap. 23: PL 50, 667–668), as presented in the Divine Office for Friday, 27th Week in Ordinary Time.

> tries, as it were, its limbs, and proves the ground under it, and feels its way. From time to time, it makes essays which fail.... In time it enters upon strange territory; points of controversy alter their bearing ... and old principles reappear under new forms. It changes with them in order to remain the same. In a higher world it is otherwise, but here below to live is to change, and to be perfect is to have changed often.[105]

He looked at daily life and the acquisition of personal knowledge and described how a consensus is achieved among human beings in judging what is true and what is not. Our own ideas regarding a specific topic always develop within the context of the ideas of others, and this interplay shapes the outcome of our thought. The development of Christian Doctrine occurs via a similar process.

The distinct, brilliant contribution of Newman is that he supplied an answer to an abstract theological problem as well as to the proliferation of creeds that was evident during his era. He provided guidance for how, when faced with rival truth claims, one can identify and embrace the proper belief. This is radically distinct from the *evolution* of doctrine — an approach that would be condemned by Pope Pius X in his 1907 encyclical *Pascendi Dominici Gregis.*[106] There is a deep chasm between evolution and development. The proposal that there is doctrinal evolution maintains that a doctrine can change, thereby making it quite different from the original doctrine and implying that nothing is either stable or immutable in Church doctrinal teachings. To the contrary, there is stability and immutability in the concept of the *development* of Christian Doctrine. Newman insisted that any kind of development that was not faithful to its original idea was a corruption

[105] Newman, *Essay on Development,* 40.

[106] Pius X, Encyclical Letter on the Doctrines of the Modernists *Pascendi Dominici Gregis* (September 8, 1907).

of truth. He proposed seven elements that can be used to distinguish between authentic development and corruption.[107]

1. Preservation of type — the substantial identity of an idea must not change: "Small are a baby's limbs, a youth's are larger, yet they are the same."

2. Continuity of principles — the permanent assumptions underlying an idea must not change: e.g., the sacramental principle, the dogmatic principle, the principle of asceticism, and so on.

3. Power of assimilation — an idea must have the capacity to absorb or incorporate external ideas: for example, the assimilation of an Aristotelian philosophical idiom by medieval theologians.

4. Logical sequence — a development must follow logically from its earlier form.

5. Anticipation of its future — an idea must anticipate its development: for example, the doctrine of the resurrection of the body anticipates the cult of saints' relics.

6. Conservative action upon its past — a development must conserve, not obscure, the content of its earlier forms.

7. Chronic vigor — a development must stand the test of time.

[107] These elements are taken from Newman, *Essay on Development*, chap. 5, "Genuine Developments Contrasted with Corruptions."

Newman's eminent theological approach showed that theological analysis demonstrated that the development of ideas within the Roman Catholic Church fulfilled these elements. Her doctrine preserved the teaching of the Apostles and Ecumenical Councils, while undergoing a gradual blossoming over time:

> At first there is a seed, and a stalk springs out of the seed, and from the stalk bursts out a shrub, and then its branches and foliage grow vigorous, and all that we mean by a tree is unfolded; then there is the swelling of the bud, and the bud is resolved into a blossom, and the blossom is opened into a fruit, and is for a while rudimental and unformed, till, by degrees following out its life, it is matured into mellowness of flavor.[108]

He concluded that the Catholic Church in all eras "is undeniably the historical continuation of the religious system, which bore the name of Catholic in the eighteenth century, in the seventeenth, in the sixteenth, and so back in every preceding century, till we arrive at the first."[109]

This personal discovery was the final step in his process of converting to Roman Catholicism. Although there is debate as to exactly when Newman adopted the principle of development,[110] it is very clear that this insight was a key impetus for his conversion.

Two Roman Pontiffs have spoken about the connection between the theory of development and Newman's personal faith. As already indicated, Pope Benedict XVI, while still Cardinal Ratzinger, drew a connection between the theory of development and Newman's own lived faith: "Throughout his entire life, Newman was a person converting, a person being transformed, and thus he always

[108] Ibid., 363.
[109] Ibid., 169.
[110] Ker, *John Henry Newman*, 45–50.

remained and became ever more himself."[111] Ian Ker states that this dimension should not be overlooked. Newman, he observes, "emphasized the real and the concrete as opposed to the notional and abstract, the personal and the experiential as opposed to the impersonal and theoretical, the theory of development extended the unfolding of his own ideas, with fidelity to his own principles, to the whole history of Christian thought."[112] It is through human activity that ideas grow. The value of Newman's work, Ratzinger wrote, is that "he taught us to think historically in theology."[113]

Pope Francis referred to Newman in his encyclical *Lumen Fidei,* when he wrote about the development of Christian Doctrine:

> The unity of faith, then, is the unity of a living body; this was clearly brought out by Blessed John Henry Newman when he listed among the characteristic notes for distinguishing the continuity of doctrine over time its power to assimilate everything that it meets in the various settings in which it becomes present and in the diverse cultures which it encounters.[114]

The same Pontiff also referred to it in his book, *My Door Is Always Open: A Conversation on Faith, Hope and the Church in a Time of Change.*[115]

Furthermore, Newman's eminent teaching anticipated and underlined the thought of the dogmatic constitution *Dei Verbum,* which described how divine revelation is handed down.[116] Newman wrote that "there is no one aspect deep enough to exhaust the contents of a

[111] Ratzinger, "Presentation on the Occasion of the First Centenary."
[112] Ker, *John Henry Newman,* 315.
[113] Ratzinger, "Presentation on the Occasion of the First Centenary."
[114] *Lumen Fidei,* no. 48.
[115] Francis, *My Door Is Always Open,* 118.
[116] See chapter 4.

real idea, no one term or proposition which will serve to define it,"[117] while simultaneously, the plurality of aspects found in so great an idea as Christianity must ultimately cohere and stay faithful to its original principles. One aspect of Revelation must not exclude or obscure another, because "Christianity is dogmatical, devotional, practical all at once; it is esoteric and exoteric; it is indulgent and strict; it is light and dark; it is love, and it is fear."[118]

Newman's relationship to the Magisterium of the Catholic Church has been covered in other sections of this book. In essence, Newman's teaching is that any Roman Pontiff exercising the *munus docendi*, the duty to teach, must draw his teaching from the deposit of faith in order to be protected by the guarantee of Papal Infallibility defined by Vatican I as binding doctrine. The sole function of this papal *munus* is to guard and expound the content of divine revelation. Thus, Papal Infallibility and the Magisterium go hand in hand and are inseparable, and they logically formed part of Newman's teaching on the development of Christian Doctrine.

Newman's private correspondence reveals that he dreaded the prospect of a definition of Papal Infallibility.[119] But this is not because he rejected the teaching: his belief in Papal Infallibility existed decades before the definition of the Dogma.[120] His letters written between January 1868 and December 1873 contain many emphatic assertions that he had always held that doctrine, though he did not rate it higher

117 *Essay on Development*, 35.

118 Ibid., 36.

119 The letters are found in volumes 24–26 of *The Letters and Diaries of John Henry Newman*, eds. Charles Stephen Dessain and Thomas Gornall, S.J. (Clarendon Press, 1973–1974).

120 Stanley L. Jaki, "Newman's Logic and the Logic of the Papacy," *Faith and Reason* 13, no. 3 (1987): 1–15, https://media.christendom.edu/wp-content/uploads/2016/08/Stanley-L.-Jaki-Newman's-Logic-and-the-Logic-of-the-Papacy.pdf.

than a theological opinion with which one could honestly disagree. He was not opposed per se to the doctrine; however, as already stated, he deemed that the timing of the Dogma was not right. In fact, Newman was proven correct because after the Dogma was defined there was a violent backlash against it from English Protestant and Anglican leaders, their congregations, and even the English secular government. This violent reaction, as stated elsewhere, did not prevent Newman from courageously stepping into the controversy, which was mainly due to prejudice, anti-Catholicism, and sheer bitterness.

He specifically acknowledged the need for Papal Infallibility in only one letter: "In the present state of the world, the Catholic body may require to be like an army in the field, under strict and immediate discipline."[121] Newman saw no conflict between a duly informed conscience and Papal Infallibility, for conscience was "not a judgment upon speculative truth, any abstract doctrine, but bears immediately upon conduct, on something to be done or not done." He appealed to St. Thomas Aquinas in writing that "conscience cannot come into direct collision with the Church's or the Pope's infallibility; which is engaged only on general propositions, or the condemnation of propositions simply particular."[122] Newman's methodical argument was rather straightforward: someone had to call the shots, and that someone was the Roman Pontiff.

Faith and Reason

The issue of the relationship between faith and reason is another major topic Newman spoke expertly about. This issue had been around for a millennium by Newman's time. He, too, wrote about it. His writings were echoed not only in Vatican II but also in the teachings of Popes

[121] *Letters and Diaries*, 24:325.
[122] *Letter to the Duke of Norfolk*, 62.

John Paul II and Benedict XVI. The key phrase is the education of the *total person*, rather than an education restricted to academic subjects.

The California Catholic Conference issued a summary of what Pope John Paul II had stated in his encyclical *Fides et Ratio* of September 14, 1998:

> The encyclical *Fides et Ratio* was written by Pope John Paul II to his fellow bishops in 1998 to address the relationship between faith and reason. It was written to support and defend traditional Christian philosophy. His Holiness believed that faith and reason together allow people to know and love God.... Truth is discovered through the interaction of faith and reason together. Both are necessary to know God; reason alone cannot result in the ultimate truth. The rise of rationalism has led some to believe in the separation of faith and reason but the result has been disastrous for the promotion of life.... The Holy Father concluded by emphasizing that God and truth are one and the same and that both reason and faith are needed to understand this certainty.[123]

Pope Benedict XVI, speaking on the writings of St. Thomas Aquinas, a theological tradition that Newman respected and utilized, stated,

> Together with the agreement between reason and faith, we must recognize on the other hand that they avail themselves of different cognitive procedures. Reason receives a truth by virtue of its intrinsic evidence, mediated or unmediated; faith, on the contrary, accepts a truth on the basis of

[123] California Catholic Conference, "Fides et Ratio (Relationship Between Faith and Reason)," January 8, 2015, https://cacatholic.org/teachings/catholic-social-teaching/fides-et-ratio-relationship-between-faith-and-reason/.

> the authority of the Word of God that is revealed.... Faith, in fact, protects reason from any temptation to distrust its own abilities, stimulates it to be open to ever broader horizons, keeps alive in it the search for foundations and, when reason itself is applied to the supernatural sphere of the relationship between God and man, faith enriches his work.... Moreover, it is not only faith that helps reason. Reason too, with its own means can do something important for faith.... Reason can recognize this by considering what it is good to do and what it is good to avoid in order to achieve that felicity which everyone has at heart, which also implies a responsibility towards others and, therefore, the search for the common good.[124]

The exposition of the logical structure of religious assent in describing the relationship between faith and reason is both highly personal and entirely rational. It is regarded as one of Newman's most important contributions to theology and education.[125]

Ian Ker deems *An Essay in Aid of a Grammar of Assent* to be a classic work of philosophy of religion: "No attempt to summarize the book can do justice to the richness of the examples adduced of variegated intellectual activity."[126] In dealing with the subject, Newman deliberately refrained from preparing himself by reading other authors so as to present his own fresh and unadulterated perspective. It was inseparable from his own experience of conversion.[127]

124 Benedict XVI, General Audience, June 16, 2010.

125 Francis Arnella Clamor, "Newman and the Search for a 'Via Media' Between Atheism and Catholicity," in *John Henry Newman: Doctor of the Church*, eds. Philippe Lefebvre and Colin Mason (Family Publications, 2007), 62.

126 Ker, *John Henry Newman*, 314.

127 *Letters and Diaries*, 24:370.

There is nothing essentially innovative in this work. James Pereiro commented that Newman's "theory of knowledge, while being highly personal, is in general agreement with Aristotelian-Thomist principles."[128] However, Cardinal Avery Dulles, S.J., comments that the conviction which directed Newman's thoughts was, "his profound and realistic theory of religious knowledge."[129] Newman's contemporary society had a mounting pluralism of religious beliefs, or even its absence. The British empirical tradition in both philosophy and theology placed religious knowledge outside the bounds of reason, limiting its scope to abstract reasoning about quantity and experimental reasoning concerning matters of fact. Furthermore, some empirical philosophers, such as the Scottish David Hume (1711–1776), entirely rejected belief in God. Others sought to free religion from the rational sphere, thereby placing faith exclusively within the field of emotion and sentiment.[130] This proposal was seen to protect faith by making it a private internal conviction, untestable, and therefore unassailable by reason. Newman provided his own theory which, as Pope Paul VI indicated, "was deeply grounded in the faith and, at the same time, was in close harmony with the best of the demands of intelligence and modern feeling."[131]

Newman's approach was far ahead of his time. He anticipated the First Vatican Council's treatment of faith and reason as mutually

[128] James Pereiro, "Newman, Tradition and Development," in *John Henry Newman: Doctor of the Church*, 249.

[129] Avery Dulles, *John Henry Newman* (Bloomsbury Academic, 2009), 58.

[130] Michael A. Dauphinais, "'Faith and Reason' in Newman: Learning to 'See Things as God Sees Them,'" in *A Guide to John Henry Newman: His Life and Thought*, ed. Juan R. Vélez (Catholic University of America Press, 2022), 288.

[131] Paul VI, "Wealth of Cardinal Newman's Thought."

supporting as stated in the dogmatic constitution *Dei Filius*.[132] Newman argued that the act of faith was entirely congruent with reason. While still an Anglican priest, during the 1830s, he expressed a wish to write "a philosophical polemic, suited to these times ... to meet the objections of infidels against the Church."[133] He took the opportunity of his *Oxford University Sermons* to outline his philosophical thought, already indicated in his previous writings, and expanded it in order to present it as a coherent system. He ultimately completed it in 1870 in *An Essay in Aid of a Grammar of Assent*.[134]

Newman confided to his friends that it took him twenty years to complete this work, written in the form of "a conversational essay."[135] Newman gave a rational account of the very complicated process through which an individual slowly advances by logical steps from atheism to theism, and eventually from that state to Catholicism. His essential idea was that religious belief must be regarded not as the departure point of certitude, but as first ensuing from an act of assent, which he defined as "the absolute acceptance of a proposition without any condition."[136] Such an assent often trails from "arguments which, taken in the letter and not in their full implicit sense, are but probabilities."[137] Newman then proceeded to provide a personal example of this. He asked, "What are the grounds for thinking that I, in my own particular case, shall die?" He held this to be a fact

[132] See Vatican I, Dogmatic Constitution on the Catholic Faith *Dei Filius* (April 24, 1870), chap. 4, https://www.papalencyclicals.net/councils/ecum20.htm.

[133] John Henry Newman, *The Letters and Diaries of John Henry Newman*, volume 14, *Papal Aggression*, eds. Charles Stephen Dessain and Vincent Ferrer Blehl (Thomas Nelson and Sons, 1963), 206.

[134] John Henry Newman, *An Essay in Aid of a Grammar of Assent* (Longmans, Green and Co., 1903).

[135] *Letters and Diaries*, 25:131.

[136] *Grammar of Assent*, 13.

[137] Ibid., 293.

with certainty, for death comes to all. Yet, Newman pointed out that he could not furnish concrete evidence for his personal demise by demonstration, any more than he could demonstrate any other future act. Rather, others could provide him with generalized evidence that every other person who has lived, but is not still alive, has died. Consequently, they could postulate a "law of death" based on observational support from natural science. However, this provided proof only by referring to past events and to the death of others; there was no strictly logical proof that, in his own specific case, Newman eventually would die like every other person. This led him to assert that his certitude rested on the strength of probability, something to which his intellect assented. Thus, Newman concluded, "what logic cannot do, my own living personal reasoning, my good sense ... does for me, and I am possessed with the most precise, absolute, masterful certitude of my dying some day or other."[138]

He insisted that the value of antecedent probability serving as the basis also applied to religious belief. He had already argued this point in *An Essay on the Development of Christian Doctrine*.[139] Newman likened this to the imagery of "a cable, which is made up of a number of separate threads, each feeble, yet together as sufficient as an iron rod."[140] This supplied the basis for conviction, which was "an assent to an assent."[141] When this was accompanied by a sense of intellectual security and a determination to persevere in one's belief, it was certitude. Certitude was either a mere conviction or indefectible: "Whoever loses his conviction on a given point is

[138] Ibid., 298–301.

[139] *Essay on Development*, 107.

[140] John Henry Newman, *The Letters and Diaries of John Henry Newman*, vol. 21: *The Apologia*, eds. Charles Stephen Dessain and Edward E. Kelly (Thomas Nelson and Sons, 1971), 146.

[141] *Grammar of Assent*, 195.

thereby proved not to have been certain of it. Certitude ought to stand all trials, or it is not certitude."[142] Certitude necessitated three conditions: "that it follows on investigation and proof, that it is accompanied by a specific sense of intellectual satisfaction and repose, and that it is irreversible." If, to the contrary, "the assent is made without rational grounds, it is a rash judgment, a fancy, or a prejudice; if without the sense of finality, it is scarcely more than an inference; if without permanence, it is a mere conviction."[143]

Newman went on to state that our religious assent did not follow a logical process because, in this instance, belief reflected "our most natural mode of reasoning, not from propositions to propositions, but from things to things, from concrete to concrete, from wholes to wholes."[144]

Once assent is conceded, the antecedent probabilities from which it first drew its conclusions lose the reason for their consideration. According to Newman, this ordinary mode of reasoning was like "a peasant who is weather-wise" and may "yet be simply unable to assign intelligible reasons why he thinks it will be fine tomorrow" — or whose reasons for thinking in this way may be unconvincing, "but that will not weaken his own confidence in his prediction"; he "does not proceed step by step, but he feels all at once and together the force of various combined phenomena."[145] It overflowed into Newton's method of finding the root of an equation: "the evidence for which rested on no other foundation than belief in Newton's sagacity until a proof was furnished over a century later." Newman used the term "Illative Sense" when referring to the

[142] Ibid., 256.
[143] Ibid., 258.
[144] Ibid., 330.
[145] Ibid., 332.

perfected intellectual faculty responsible for "the sole and final judgment on the validity of an inference in concrete matter."[146]

This sense is "a sort of instinct or inspiration" that "attends upon the whole course of thought from antecedents to consequents, with a minute diligence and unwearied presence."[147] It acts as the decisive test of truth and error in human inferences.[148] It is the faculty that allowed Newman "to prove Christianity in the same informal way in which I can prove for certain that I have been born into this world, and that I shall die out of it."[149] Newman regarded faith as an act aided by reason. Thus, many of his efforts were directed towards the cultivation of the intellect.

Conscience

Another eminent teaching of Newman regarded the role of one's conscience. It has already been stated earlier that a number of Popes spoke about Newman's great contribution to this subject. Newman addressed it publicly for the first time in his homily at the Oxford University Church of St. Mary's on Easter Tuesday, April 13, 1830. The topic appeared again in *An Essay on the Development of Christian Doctrine.*[150] He explained during his homily that we first encounter the Creator not through revealed religion but through the "inward law of Conscience." In other words, our experience is radically different from the one St. Paul received on his way to Damascus (Acts 9:3–5). Our personal conscience supplies us with the elements of a religious system that is entirely natural, though it is of divine origin. This claim is rooted in the Old Testament, when the prophet Jeremiah affirmed in the name of Yahweh: "The Lord declares: I will put my law within them,

[146] Ibid., 345.
[147] Ibid., 358, 362.
[148] Ibid., 345, 359.
[149] Ibid., 411.
[150] *Essay on Development,* 48.

and I will write it on their hearts. And I will be their God, and they shall be my people" (Jer. 31:33; see also Ps. 37:31). It is reiterated in the Letter to the Hebrews (8:10 and 10:16).

The inward role of conscience precedes any reception of revealed truth, though it is perfected by Divine Revelation. Newman maintained that conscience "is the essential principle and sanction of Religion in the mind."[151] He asserted in his *Essay on the Development of Doctrine* that there were times when inward sentiments imply the real existence of an external object: "Conscience, the existence of which we cannot deny, is a proof of the doctrine of a Moral Governor, which alone gives it a meaning and scope."[152]

However, his fullest treatment of the subject came many years later. It is found in the book-length *Letter to the Duke of Norfolk*, published in 1875. By this time, Newman had been a Catholic for many years. The letter, formally addressed to the Duke of Norfolk, his friend and former student, was actually directed at the views of Prime Minister William Gladstone (1809–1898). Gladstone scoffed at and ridiculed the Dogma of Papal Infallibility,[153] which had been defined during Vatican I. Newman explained that the Roman Pontiff "is not inspired; he has no inherent gift of divine knowledge, but when he speaks ex Cathedra, he may say little or much, but he is simply protected from saying what is untrue."[154] The occasion also served as an opportunity to diplomatically criticize Catholic extremists, the Ultramontanes.[155]

[151] John Henry Newman, *Fifteen Sermons Preached Before the University of Oxford Between A.D. 1826 and 1843* (Longmans, Green and Co., 1909), 19.

[152] *Essay on Development,* 48.

[153] William Ewart Gladstone, *The Vatican Decrees in Their Bearing on Civil Allegiance: A Political Expostulation* (London, 1874), 12.

[154] Quoted in Wilfrid Ward, *The Life of Cardinal Newman Based on His Private Journals and Correspondence,* vol. 1 (Longmans, Green and Co., 1912), 378.

[155] Some Catholic extremists maintained that a Pope was infallible even in his private opinions.

Newman insisted that Roman Catholics were genuine British citizens. This was important because Catholics were being unjustly accused of owing their primary civil allegiance to the bishop of Rome and not to their homeland — something which was absolutely false. He first presented an outline of the history of papal authority and explained how far this went in the life of the Catholic believer. The Roman Pontiff enjoyed authority over faith and morals, though even in this area the Catholic did not depend mainly on papal pronouncements but "on the three Christian foundations of Faith, Hope, and Charity, on the Ten Commandments, and on the six Precepts of the Church." Indeed, Newman contended, "so little does the Pope come into this whole system of moral theology by which (as by our conscience) our lives are regulated, that the weight of his hand upon us, as private men, is absolutely unappreciable, and thus, the matter must be first referred to the individual conscience."[156]

Newman taught that conscience is "the voice of God in the nature and heart of man, as distinct from the voice of Revelation"; it is "a constituent element of the mind" and "the internal witness of both the existence and law of God" because the voice of conscience is as magisterial as it is fundamental to our nature. It is, he continued, "the aboriginal Vicar of Christ, a prophet in its informations, a monarch in its peremptoriness, a priest in its blessings and anathemas, and, even though the eternal priesthood throughout the Church could cease to be, in it the sacerdotal principle would remain and would have a sway."[157]

Therefore, conscience for Newman was not impartial with respect to being a principle of private judgment, though it was an inner principle of authority. Thus, it required authority as its

[156] *Letter to the Duke of Norfolk*, 229, 232–233.

[157] Ibid., 248–249.

counterpart.[158] He identified these two elements in his *Essay in Aid of a Grammar of Assent* as "a moral sense, and a sense of duty; a judgment of the reason and a magisterial dictate."[159]

Newman's distinct contribution in his treatment of conscience was his emphasis on this "double aspect," wherein an internal judgment of right and wrong cooperates with the external demands of the divine law and its magisterial expression. This understanding of conscience was consistent with both the Thomistic tradition specifically[160] and the Church's theological tradition more generally. The influence of Newman's writings on conscience is evident in the fifty-two references to conscience in the documents of the Second Vatican Council.[161] It should be noted that his teaching formed a central pillar of the conciliar declaration on religious freedom, *Dignitatis Humanae*:

> On his part, man perceives and acknowledges the imperatives of the divine law through the mediation of conscience. In all his activity a man is bound to follow his conscience in order that he may come to God, the end and purpose of life. It follows that he is not to be forced to act in a manner contrary to his conscience. Nor, on the other hand, is he to be restrained from acting in accordance with his conscience, especially in matters religious. The reason is that the

158 Charlotte Hansen, "Newman, Conscience and Authority," *New Blackfriars* 92, no. 1038 (2011): 222.

159 *Grammar of Assent*, 105.

160 See, for example, Thomas Aquinas, *Summa Theologica* I, q. 79, art. 13; and I-II, q. 19. art. 5.

161 Anthony Fisher, O.P., "Conscience, Relativism and Truth: The Witness of Newman," address to Conference on Newman the Prophet: A Saint for Our Times, Pontifical University of St. Thomas, Rome, posted at Catholic Archdiocese of Sydney, https://www.sydneycatholic.org/addresses-and-statements/2019/conscience-relativism-and-truth-the-witness-of-newman/.

> exercise of religion, of its very nature, consists before all else in those internal, voluntary and free acts whereby man sets the course of his life directly toward God.[162]

Thus, the freedom to follow one's conscience stands alongside the admonition that it must be properly formed and the believer must carefully take into account the firm doctrine of the Catholic Church. This was not only very important to Newman's contemporaries; it is also applicable to the Church of today, when subjectivism is paramount in society. Pope Francis refers to this sad state of affairs when commenting, "The contemporary world risks confusing the primacy of the conscience, which is always to be respected, with the exclusive autonomy of the individual."[163]

The Laity

Newman also wrote eminently about the role of the laity, an extremely important subject in our contemporary Church.

Newman republished his Anglican *Lectures on the Prophetical Office of the Church* in 1877.[164] He added a preface in this third publication, in which he refuted the criticisms of the Catholic Church contained in the original publication.[165] Eamon Duffy, subtly alluding to Newman's sheer intellectual honesty and integrity, describes the preface as "a self-conscious corrective to nineteenth-century

[162] Vatican II, Declaration on Religious Freedom *Dignitatis Humanae* (December 7, 1965), in *Vatican Council II: The Conciliar and Post Conciliar Documents*, ed. Austin Flannery (Liturgical Press, 1975), no. 3.

[163] Francis, "Video Message to Participants in the 3rd International Symposium on the Apostolic Exhortation 'Amoris Laetitia,'" (transcript), November 11, 2017.

[164] *Lectures on the Prophetical Office of the Church* was originally published in 1837.

[165] John Henry Newman, *Lectures on the Prophetical Office of the Church, The Via Media of the Anglican Church* (Longmans, Green and Co., 1901), vol. 1, ix.

ultramontane ecclesiology, written from within, though the originality of the corrective was to have a life and value far beyond the occasions and the problems which evoked it.[166]

It was corrective not only to his own original work but also to the prevailing "monolithic" view of the Church of his day. Newman described the Church in terms of Christ's threefold Office of Priest, Prophet, and King, simultaneously representing "a philosophy, a political power, and a religious rite."[167] The Prophetical Office signified the Church as teacher, the Priestly Office was the Church in prayer, and the Regal Office was the Church as governing. This idea was first expressed in the scholastic tradition, referenced in the *Catechism of the Council of Trent,* and found its first magisterial expression in Pope Pius XII's encyclical *Mystici Corporis.*[168] Contrasted with a view of the Church "in which hierarchy or governance determine all aspects of religious life," Newman's ecclesiology is rich, dynamic, and true to "the lived reality of historic Christianity."[169]

Throughout her history, Newman observed, the Roman Catholic Church has consistently balanced these three Offices: "Each of the three has its separate scope and direction; each has its own interests to promote and further; each has to find room for the claims of the other two; and each will find its own line of action influenced and modified by the others."[170]

Newman manifested his deep knowledge of Church history and the interrelatedness of these three Offices by recognizing instances

166 Eamon Duffy, "'That Was Then, This Is Now': Some Comments on Newman's 1877 Preface to the 'Via Media' and the Modern Church," *New Blackfriars* 92, no. 1038 (2011): 170.

167 Ibid., 171; Newman, *Prophetical Office,* xl.

168 Peter Phillips, "Newman, Vatican II, and the Triple Office," *New Blackfriars* 94, no. 1049 (2013): 108.

169 Duffy, "'That Was Then," 171, 173.

170 Newman, *Prophetical Office,* xli.

when the Teaching Office of the Church was "impeded for a while in its action ... by the remonstrances of charity and of the spirit of peace," such as by leaving a point of doctrine temporarily undefined.[171] On the other hand, the Priestly Office of the Church is exercised when she makes determinations on private revelations and popular devotions. Furthermore, there are occasions when the Governing Office must supply what is absent or insufficient in the other two Offices. These actions provide a guarantee "that no act could be theologically an error, which was absolutely and undeniably necessary for the unity, sanctity, and peace of the Church."[172]

He gave apostolic succession as an example, writing of "our certainty that the Apostolical succession of Bishops in the Catholic Church has no flaw in it, and that the validity of the Sacraments is secure, in spite of possible mistakes and informalities in the course of 1800 years." This certainty "rests upon our faith that He who has decreed the end has decreed the means,—that He is always sufficient for His Church,—that, if He has given us a promise ever to be with us, He will perform it."[173]

When speaking of the Threefold Office, Newman spoke principally of the Body of Christ as a whole. His definition presumed, though it did not limit itself to, the hierarchical aspect of the Church. His understanding of the role of the laity was way ahead of his time. Yves Congar, almost a century later and before the assembling of the Second Vatican Council, stated, "With Newman—and not that he was the only one, but he was and remains to this day the *locus classicus* of the question—the idea of development became an inner dimension of that tradition. He made a decisive contribution to the problem of the relationship between magisterium and history in

[171] Ibid., l.

[172] Ibid., lxxxiv–xv.

[173] Ibid., lxxxiv–xv.

tradition."[174] Already in 1957, Congar had made a decisive contribution to the problem by bringing the role of the laity into clearer focus, drawing on the imagery of the Threefold Office.[175] Newman's writings had earlier spoken of the laity as a source of a genuine agency within the Church, and this at a time when the common view of lay involvement was mute.

Newman's heightened awareness of the role of the laity in the Church was the result of his study, analysis, and insights into the historical condition of the Church in the fourth century at the time of the Arian heresy concerning the true identity of Jesus Christ as being truly God and truly man. Arianism denied the divinity of Christ. The Council of Nicaea condemned this teaching in 325 and reaffirmed the apostolic understanding of Jesus Christ as truly God and truly man, of the same substance as God the Father and eternally existing with Him.[176] Despite this condemnation, many Catholic bishops of that era went over to Arianism. But the laity had an instinct for the truth and resisted Arian bishops while supporting those Catholic bishops who refuted the heresy. Arians were finally expelled from the Church by the First Council of Constantinople in 381.[177]

One day, Bishop William Bernard Ullathorne, O.S.B., Newman's bishop, asked: "Who are the laity?" Newman noted that, "I answered (not in these words) that the Church would look foolish

[174] Yves M. J. Congar, O.P., *Tradition and Traditions: An Historical and a Theological Essay* (Macmillan, 1967), 211.

[175] Yves M. J. Congar, O.P., *Lay People in the Church: A Study for a Theology of Laity*, trans. Donald Attwater (Geoffrey Chapman, 1957).

[176] See *Catechism of the Catholic Church*, no. 465, which cites Council of Nicaea I (325), DS 130, 126.

[177] Lewis Ayres, *Nicaea and its Legacy: An Approach to Fourth-Century Trinitarian Theology* (Oxford University Press, 2006).

without them."[178] This was very telling. Newman's understanding of the Church could not be separated from his view of the laity. It was expressed in his article in *The Rambler* magazine, "On Consulting the Faithful in Matters of Doctrine," published in July 1859, the first issue of Newman's editorship. Though dogmatically sound, it turned out to be very controversial. He wrote about the faithful being consulted prior to the dogmatic definition of the Immaculate Conception in December 1854.[179] This immediately drew accusations of being almost heretical. Consequently, Newman resigned the editorship, but not before offering his position in his second and final issue of the magazine.

He stated that the laity must be consulted because "the body of the faithful is one of the witnesses to the fact of the tradition of revealed doctrine, and because their consensus through Christendom is the voice of the Infallible Church."[180] He made it clear that doctrine was not based on any democratic principle; rather, "Consulting the Faithful" expressed the developed theological concept of *sensus fidelium*.[181] The problem lay in the interpretation of the term *sensus*. Its ordinary usage in the English language denotes a private opinion, while the theological meaning in Latin follows its Thomistic interpretation. This teaching had been elaborated already in the sixteenth century by the Dominican theologian Melchior Cano (1509–1560), who described it as a "baptismal instinct" whereby individual

[178] *On Consulting the Faithful in Matters of Doctrine*, edited with an introduction by John Coulson (Rowman and Littlefield Publishers, 1961), 41.

[179] Pius IX, Apostolic Constitution on the Immaculate Conception *Ineffabilis Deus* (December 8, 1854).

[180] Newman, "On Consulting the Faithful in Matters of Doctrine," *The Rambler* (July 1859): 205.

[181] Edward Miller, "Newman's Teaching on the Sense of the Faithful," in *John Henry Newman: Doctor of the Church*, 145.

Christians could distinguish between true and false doctrine.[182] Newman put forward a practical example: "A physician consults the pulse of his patient, but not in the same sense in which his patient consults him. It is but an index of the state of his health." Similarly, the Church hierarchy does not ask the faithful their opinion on matters of doctrine, but merely "consults" the fact of their belief "as a testimony to that apostolical tradition, on which alone any doctrine whatsoever can be defined.[183] In other words, the *sensus* or *consensus* of the faithful acts as a testimony to the authentic doctrine of the Church.

The principle of the *sensus fidelium* first came to Newman during his studies for the priesthood in Rome in 1847 as the solution to a problem. He received the idea from the Jesuit theologian Giovanni Perrone (1794–1876), who showed how, even when belief in a doctrine was not sufficiently evidenced among the bishops and theologians of the early Church, "the voice of tradition may in certain cases express itself, not by Councils, nor Fathers, nor Bishops, but the '*communis fidelium sensus*.' "[184] Miller comments that it was Newman who expressed the idea of the *sensus fidelium,* "in its fully active sense": the baptized faithful are not merely passive recipients of the hierarchical teaching but "a robust actor on its own behalf, capable of recognizing and rejecting doctrinal corruptions."[185]

As such, "although Newman inherits the term *sensus fidelium,* he as much as anyone can be credited with retrieving it for productive currency in Catholic thinking, such as happened at the Second Vatican Council."[186] Newman's teaching featured prominently in the conciliar dogmatic constitution on the Church, *Lumen Gentium,* as

[182] Ibid., 146.
[183] Newman, "On Consulting the Faithful," 199.
[184] Ibid., 214.
[185] Miller, "Newman's Teaching," 155
[186] Ibid., 147.

already stated (see chapter 4). The conciliar teaching extended the scope of Newman's thought by recognizing that the laity themselves can exercise a teaching function, alongside the hierarchy, in their respective vocations.[187] This development clamored for a particular emphasis on Newman's description of the laity as being witnesses to a revealed and received doctrine.

To return momentarily to the beginning of the topic, Newman illustrated in his portrayal of the Arian crisis how "the divine dogma of our Lord's divinity was proclaimed, enforced, maintained, and (humanly speaking) preserved, far more by the 'Ecclesia docta' [the taught Church] than by the 'Ecclesia docens' [the teaching Church]."[188]

This claim necessitated the preexistence of an *Ecclesia docta*. The inverse consultation of an *Ecclesia indocta* would hardly witness to the tradition of the Apostles. Thus, there must be clarity of teaching and an authentic engagement with the truths of the Faith to enable the laity to exercise their important duty of upholding them. In the same way, as Miller rightly observes, the Bishops of the Church, though they are the proper teachers of the Faith, are no more its sources than are the faithful.[189] Both are liberated and constrained by the same confines of divine revelation. The *sensus fidelium* assumes faithfulness to a received teaching, as Newman stated: "Commonly the Church has nothing more to do than to go on in her own proper duties, in confidence and peace; to stand still and to see the salvation of God. 'The meek shall inherit the land and delight themselves in abundant peace.' "[190]

[187] See, for example, Gerald O'Collins, "Laity as Teachers in the *Ecclesia Docens*," *Irish Theological Quarterly* 86, no. 3 (2021): 241–253.

[188] Newman, "On Consulting the Faithful," 213.

[189] Miller, "Newman's Teaching," 148.

[190] "The Biglietto Speech," May 12, 1879, as quoted in *L'Osservatore Romano*, Weekly Edition in English, April 14, 2010, 9, https://www.ewtn.com/catholicism/library/biglietto-speech-5245.

EDUCATION

Another eminent topic for Newman was the role of education, specifically Catholic education. Newman regarded faith as an act aided by reason. Thus, many of his efforts were directed toward the cultivation of the intellect. He enjoyed considerable influence in this field.[191]

There is no stretch of imagination in perceiving John Henry Newman as a great educator. It was the year 1854, a decade after his conversion, when a movement spearheaded by Archbishop (later Cardinal) Paul Cullen of Dublin (1803–1878) and led by Fr. John Henry Newman succeeded in opening the doors of a new Catholic University of Ireland (now known as University College Dublin). Its purpose was to make higher education accessible to a broad sweep of Irish people. The university opened its doors on November 3, 1854. Newman served as its first rector, an assignment that lasted four years. Next, in 1859, he founded the Oratory School in Woodcote, some six miles north of Reading, England. He based it on the model of contemporary English public schools (the equivalent of "private" schools in the United States) to provide a liberal education for Catholic boys.

Newman published a volume of lectures entitled *The Idea of a University*, explaining his philosophy of education. He spelled out his vision of establishing an educational institution that acts as "an Alma Mater, knowing her children one by one, not a foundry, or a mint, or a treadmill."[192] It contained a defense of liberal education as an end in itself:

[191] See the works authored or edited by Paul Shrimpton. *A Catholic Eton? Newman's Oratory School* (Gracewing, 2005); *The "Making of Men": The Idea and Reality of Newman's University in Oxford and Dublin* (Gracewing, 2014); *My Campaign in Ireland,* vol. 1, *Catholic University Reports and Other Papers* (Gracewing, 2021), and *My Campaign in Ireland,* vol. 2, *My Connection with the Catholic University* (Gracewing, 2022).

[192] John Henry Newman, *The Idea of a University* (Longmans, Green and Co., 1907), 144–145.

> To open the mind, to correct it, to refine it, to enable it to know, and to digest, master, rule, and use its knowledge, to give it power over its own faculties, application, flexibility, method, critical exactness, sagacity, resource, address, eloquent expression, is ... an object as intelligible as the cultivation of virtue, while, at the same time, it is absolutely distinct from it.[193]

His idea encountered much resistance — another instance indicating that his teaching was far ahead of his time. He advocated what has been described as a middle way "between an obscurantism which tramples on the rights of knowledge and Free-Thought which will not hear of the rights of revelation."[194] Consequently, he wanted to establish a Catholic university that was radically different from both the formerly Catholic universities on the European continent that had been recently secularized and from Protestant English-speaking universities. He wrote,

> A University, taken in its bare idea, and before we view it as an instrument of the Church, has this object and this mission; it contemplates neither moral impression nor mechanical production; it professes to exercise the mind neither in art nor in duty; its function is intellectual culture; here it may leave its scholars, and it has done its work when it has done as much as this. It educates the intellect to reason well in all matters, to reach out towards truth, and to grasp it.[195]

At the same time, the university, concerned with the whole of truth, could not omit the study of God from its purview. Theology must be

[193] Ibid., 122–123.

[194] William Barry, "John Henry Newman," *Catholic Encyclopedia*, vol. 10, ed. Charles Herbermann (Robert Appleton Company, 1911).

[195] *Idea of a University*, 125–126.

central to university education, because God is central to human existence. "How can we investigate any part of any order of Knowledge, and stop short of that which enters into every order?" Newman asked. "All true principles run over with it, all phenomena converge to it; it is truly the First and the Last."[196] In other words, Newman was promoting a new approach to teach university students from a Catholic perspective, greatly contributing to what constitutes a *Catholic* university. However, as already stated, this philosophy of a Catholic education encountered much opposition within the Irish Catholic hierarchy, beginning with, of all people, Archbishop Cullen, who wrote to the Vatican's Sacred Congregation for the Propagation of the Faith (now the Dicastery for Evangelization), criticizing Newman's lenient approach to discipline among the students.[197] Still, though Newman's approach was roundly criticized, his book on the subject exerted wide influence.[198]

Newman's influence on education was both practical and theoretical. It has already been stated that it had begun during his Anglican years as a tutor at Oxford, where he introduced the tutorial system which still continues today as a defining characteristic of the university. It played a central role in the university's intellectual revival in the nineteenth century. He regarded the proper role of the tutor as being responsible not only for the academic progress of his students but also for their moral formation.[199] At the heart of his educational outlook were the individual friendships captured in his motto as a cardinal, *Cor ad cor loquitur*.

[196] Ibid., 26.

[197] See John Cornwell, *Newman's Unquiet Grave: The Reluctant Saint* (Continuum, 2010), chap. 11.

[198] Shrimpton, *A Catholic Eton?*, 26, 29, 41–43.

[199] Paul Shrimpton, "Newman the Educator, 'From First to Last,'" in *A Guide to John Henry Newman*, 193–196.

Pope John Paul II, as stated elsewhere, commented that Newman "belongs to every time and place and people."[200] It is surely the case that this philosopher of religion and educator belongs especially to the age of critical inquiry in which we live. His *Grammar of Assent*, together with *Fifteen Sermons Preached Before the University of Oxford Between A.D. 1826 and 1843*, showed that faith did not, as some claimed, arrive at truth independently from or in opposition to reason. Belief is fundamentally rational, and faith and reason must not be placed in opposition to one another. To think and reason are as essential to us as to feel or breathe. This faculty, which affords us the dignity of creatures capable of union with God, must not be restricted to mundane things, but lifted up and perfected. Newman asserted, "We attain to heaven by using this world well, though it is to pass away; we perfect our nature, not by undoing it, but by adding to it what is more than nature, and directing it towards aims higher than its own."[201]

It might be said that what John Henry Newman was doing was following the exhortation of St. Paul to the Philippians: "Beloved, whatever is true, whatever is honorable, whatever is just, whatever is pure, whatever is pleasing, whatever is commendable, if there is any excellence and if there is anything worthy of praise, think about these things" (4:8, 9).

St. John Henry Cardinal Newman, Doctor of the Universal Church, pray for us!

[200] John Paul II, "Letter on the Occasion of the 2nd Centenary of the Birth of Cardinal John Henry Newman," January 22, 2001.

[201] *Idea of a University,* 123.

Highlights of Cardinal Newman's Life

1801: February 21, born in London

1801: April 9, baptized in the Church of England, in the Church of St. Benet Fink

1816: first major illness; at age 15, first religious conversion; converts to Evangelical Christianity, a branch of the Church of England

1816: temporarily converts to an evangelical Calvinism; believes the Pope is the antichrist

1817: at age 16, becomes an undergraduate at Trinity College, Oxford University

1822: January 11, decides to be a clergyman

1822: April 12, elected as fellow at Oriel College, Oxford University

1824: June 13, ordained an Anglican deacon; begins preaching ministry

1825: May 29, ordained an Anglican priest

1825–1826: vice-principal at St. Alban's Hall and priest at St. Clement Church in Oxford

1826: tutor at Oriel College, Oxford University

1827: preacher in Whitehall; second major illness

1828: January 5, death of youngest and favorite sister, Mary

1828: February 22, death of mentor Walter Mayers

1828: appointed vicar at St. Mary's Oxford University Church, with the benefice of Littlemore

1830: leadership at Oriel College refuses to provide him with more students

1830: begins preaching at St. Mary's Oxford University Church

1830: discovers the Church Fathers in his readings

1831–1832: select preacher at Oxford University

1832: December, Mediterranean tour

1833: falls gravely ill in Sicily (third major illness)

1833: second conversion; feels called to a mission in England

1833: composes famous poem, *Lead Kindly Light*; July 9, returns to Oxford

1833: July 14, John Keble preaches homily "National Apostasy"; it catches Newman's attention and changes his life's mission

1833: beginning of the Oxford Movement and efforts to renew and reform the Anglican Church

1833: publishes *The Arians of the Fourth Century*

1833–1841: publishes *Tracts for the Times*

1836–1839: influence in Oxford becomes notable and is considered a dangerous High Church Anglican controversialist

1841: publishes *Tract 90*; concludes the defining doctrines of the Church of England were fundamentally more Roman Catholic than Protestant; produces a very negative reaction from leaders at Oxford University

1841: resigns from Oxford University

1842: withdraws to Littlemore, outside Oxford, for prayer and study

1843: resigns as preacher at Oxford University Church of St. Mary

1843: publishes *Oxford University Sermons* and *Sermons on Subjects of the Day*

1843: September 25, preaches his last Anglican homily at Littlemore

1843: begins to consider Church of Rome as authentic Catholic Church

1845: finishes analyzing and confronting difficulties with the Church of Rome

1845: publishes *An Essay on the Development of Christian Doctrine* and *Retraction of Anti-Catholic Statements*

1845: realizes continued adherence to Anglican Church untenable, resigns

1845: ceases to be a fellow at Oxford University

1845: October 9, converts to Roman Catholicism (third conversion)

1846: sent to Rome for further studies to become Roman Catholic priest

1847: May 30, ordained a Catholic priest in Rome

1847: returns to England as an Oratorian at the end of the year

1848: February 1, establishes the Oratory of Birmingham

1849: with Fr. Frederick Faber, establishes the Oratory of London

1850: September 29, Pope Pius IX restores English Roman Catholic hierarchy

1852: June 24, found guilty of libel at the Achilli trial

1852: publishes *The Idea of a University*

1852: accepts invitation to give a series of lectures in Dublin, Ireland

1854: cofounder and first rector of the new Catholic University of Dublin (today's University College Dublin)

1858: due to conflicts over university, resigns as rector and returns to Birmingham Oratory

1859: publishes "On Consulting the Faithful in Matters of Christian Doctrine"

1859–1878: Rome investigates Newman's writings, but never condemns any of them

1864: publishes *Apologia Pro Vita Sua,* in defense of conversion journey

1868: turns down multiple invitations to serve as a theological expert at the upcoming Vatican Council I

1870: publishes *Grammar of Assent*

1874: writes *Letter to the Duke of Norfolk,* defending loyalty of Catholic to British civil government and England against criticism of Prime Minister William Gladstone

1877: returns to Oxford after thirty-four-year absence

1877: Oxford University welcomes back the son it had abandoned; receives honorary fellowship from Trinity College

1879: May 12, named a cardinal by Pope Leo XIII

1889: celebrates last Mass on Christmas Day

1890: August 11, dies of pneumonia at Birmingham Oratory

1991: January 22, declared Venerable by Pope John Paul II

2010: September 19, beatified by Pope Benedict XVI in Birmingham, England

2019: October 19, canonized by Pope Francis

2025: declared a Doctor of the Universal Church by Pope Leo XIV

Bibliography

Ayres, Lewis. *Nicaea and its Legacy: An Approach to Fourth-Century Trinitarian Theology*. Oxford University Press, 2006.

Barry, William. "John Henry Newman." In *Catholic Encyclopedia*, vol. 10. Edited by Charles Herbermann. Robert Appleton Company, 1911).

California Catholic Conference. "Fides et Ratio (Relationship Between Faith and Reason)," January 8, 2015. https://cacatholic.org/teachings/catholic-social-teaching/fides-et-ratio-relationship-between-faith-and-reason/.

Chadwick, Owen. *Acton and History.* Cambridge University Press, 2002.

Clamor, Francis Arnella. "Newman and the Search for a 'Via Media' Between Atheism and Catholicity." In *John Henry Newman: Doctor of the Church*. Edited by Philippe Lefebvre and Colin Mason. Family Publications, 2007.

Congar, Yves M. J., O.P. *Lay People in the Church: A Study for a Theology of Laity*. Translated by Donald Attwater. Geoffrey Chapman, 1957.

Congar, Yves M. J., O.P. *Tradition and Traditions: An Historical and a Theological Essay*. Macmillan, 1967.

Congregation for the Doctrine of the Faith. *Letter "Iuvenescit Ecclesia" to the Bishops of the Catholic Church Regarding the Relationship Between Hierarchical and Charismatic Gifts in the Life and the Mission of the Church*. May 15, 2016.

Connolly, John R. *John Henry Newman: A View of Catholic Faith for the New Millennium*. Rowman and Littlefield, 2005.

Cornwell, John. *Newman's Unquiet Grave: The Reluctant Saint.* Continuum, 2010.

Dauphinais, Michael A. " 'Faith and Reason' in Newman: Learning to 'See Things as God Sees Them.' " In *A Guide to John Henry Newman: His Life and Thought.* Edited by Juan R. Vélez. Catholic University of America Press, 2022.

Duffy, Eamon. "A Hero of the Church." Review of *Newman's Unquiet Grave* by John Cornwell. *New York Times Review of Books,* December 23, 2010.

Duffy, Eamon. " 'That Was Then, This Is Now': Some Comments on Newman's 1877 Preface to the 'Via Media' and the Modern Church." *New Blackfriars* 92, no. 1038 (March 2011): 170–175. https://doi.org/10.1111/j.1741-2005.2010.01409.x.

Duffy, Eamon. *The Stripping of the Altars*. Yale University Press, 1992.

Dulles, Avery. *John Henry Newman*. Bloomsbury Academic, 2009.

Ecclesiastical History Society. "Achilli v. Newman: Anti-Catholicism in Court." October 18, 2018. https://eccleshistsoc.wordpress.com/2018/10/18/achilli-v-newman-anti-catholicism-in-court/.

Fisher, Anthony, O.P. "Conscience, Relativism and Truth: The Witness of Newman." Address to Conference on Newman the Prophet: A Saint for Our Times, Pontifical University of St. Thomas, Rome. Catholic Archdiocese of Sydney. https://www.sydneycatholic.org/addresses-and-statements/2019/conscience-relativism-and-truth-the-witness-of-newman/.

Flannery, Austin, ed. *Vatican Council II: The Conciliar and Post Conciliar Documents*. Liturgical Press, 1975.

Gilley, Sheridan. *Newman and His Age.* Darton, Longman, and Todd, 2003.

Gladstone, William Ewart. *The Vatican Decrees in Their Bearing on Civil Allegiance: A Political Expostulation*. London, 1874.

Hansen, Charlotte. "Newman, Conscience and Authority." *New Blackfriars* 92, no. 1038 (February 2011): 209–223. https://doi.org/10.1111/j.1741-2005.2010.01411.x.

Hirschmann, Nancy J. *Gender, Class, and Freedom in Modern Political Theory*. Princeton University Press, 2009.

Hutton, Arthur Wollaston. "Newman, John Henry." In *Encyclopedia Britannica*, 11th ed., vol. 19. Edited by Hugh Chisholm. Cambridge University Press, 1911.

Jaki, Stanley L. "Newman's Logic and the Logic of the Papacy." *Faith and Reason* 13, no. 3 (1987): 1–15. https://media.christendom.edu/wp-content/uploads/2016/08/Stanley-L.-Jaki-Newman's-Logic-and-the-Logic-of-the-Papacy.pdf.

Jaki, Stanley L. *Conscience and Papacy.* Real View Books, 2002.

Jennings, Peter, ed. *Benedict XVI and Cardinal Newman.* Family Publications, 2005.

Ker, Ian. *John Henry Newman: A Biography.* Oxford University Press, 1988.

Lenczowski, John. "Public Diplomacy and the Lessons of the Soviet Collapse: the Record and its Implications." *Journal of Cold War Studies* 6, no. 1 (Winter 2004): 75–89. https://www.jstor.org/stable/26925348.

Miller, Edward. "Newman's Teaching on the Sense of the Faithful." In *John Henry Newman: Doctor of the Church.* Edited by Philippe Lefebvre and Colin Mason. Family Publications, 2007.

Mockler, Anthony. *John Henry Newman, Fighter, Convert and Cardinal.* Signal Books Limited, 2010.

Müller, Gerhard Ludwig. "The Call to Communion: *Anglicanorum coetibus* and Ecclesial Unity." Symposium on the Ordinariate of the Chair of St. Peter, St. Mary's Seminary, Houston, Texas, February 2, 2013. https://press.vatican.va/roman_curia/congregations/cfaith/muller/rc_con_cfaith_doc_20130202_anglicanorum-coetibus_en.html.

Newman, John Henry. *Apologia Pro Vita Sua.* London, 1864.

Newman, John Henry. *An Essay in Aid of a Grammar of Assent.* Longmans, Green and Co., 1903.

Newman, John Henry. *An Essay on the Development of Christian Doctrine.* London, 1845.

Newman, John Henry. *Fifteen Sermons Preached Before the University of Oxford Between A.D. 1826 and 1843.* Longmans, Green and Co., 1909.

Newman, John Henry. *The Idea of a University.* London: Longmans, Green and Co., 1907.

Newman, John Henry. *Lectures on the Present Position of Catholic in England, Addressed to the Brothers of the Oratory in the Summer of 1851.* Longmans, Green and Co., 1908.

Newman, John Henry. *Lectures on the Prophetical Office of the Church, The Via Media of the Anglican Church,* vol. 1. Longmans, Green and Co., 1901.

Newman, John Henry. *Letter to the Duke of Norfolk.* London: B. M. Pickering, 1895.

Newman, John Henry. *The Letters and Diaries of John Henry Newman,* vols 24–26. Clarendon Press, 1973–1974.

Newman, John Henry. *My Campaign in Ireland,* vol. 1: *Catholic University Reports and Other Papers.* Edited by Paul Shrimpton. Gracewing, 2021.

Newman, John Henry. *My Campaign in Ireland,* vol. 2: *My Connection with the Catholic University.* Edited by Paul Shrimpton. Gracewing, 2022.

Newman, John Henry. "On Consulting the Faithful in Matters of Doctrine." *The Rambler.* July 1859.

Newsome, David. *The Convert Cardinals: Newman and Manning.* First Edition, 1993.

Nichols, Aidan, O.P. *The Thought of Pope Benedict XVI: An Introduction to the Theology of Joseph Ratzinger.* Burns and Oates, 2007.

O'Collins, Gerald. "Laity as Teachers in the *Ecclesia Docens*." *Irish Theological Quarterly* 86, no. 3 (2021): 241–253, https://doi.org/10.1177/00211400211017691.

"Oxford Movement, The." In *An Episcopal Dictionary of the Church*. Edited by Robert Boak Slocum and Don S. Armentrout. Church Publishing, 2000. https://www.episcopalchurch.org/glossary/oxford-movement-the/.

Paz D. G. *Popular Anti-Catholicism in Mid-Victorian England*. Stanford University Press, 1992.

Pereiro, James. "Newman, Tradition and Development." In *John Henry Newman: Doctor of the Church*. Edited by Philippe Lefebvre and Colin Mason. Family Publications, 2007.

Phillips, Peter. "Newman, Vatican II, and the Triple Office." *New Blackfriars* 94, no. 1049 (2013): 97–112. https://doi.org/10.1111/j.1741-2005.2012.01491.x.

Ratzinger, Cardinal Joseph. "Presentation on the Occasion of the First Centenary of the Death of Card. John Henry Newman." Rome, April 28, 1990. https://www.vatican.va/roman_curia/congregations/cfaith/documents/rc_con_cfaith_doc_19900428_ratzinger-newman_en.html.

Vincent of Lérins. "The Commonitory of Vincent of Lérins." Translated by Charles A. Heurtley. In *Sulpitius Severus, Vincent of Lérins, John Cassian: A Select Library of the Nicene and Post-Nicene Fathers of the Church*. Vol. 11, edited by Schaffer, Philip and Henry Wace. New York, 1894.

Shrimpton, Paul. *A Catholic Eton? Newman's Oratory School*. Gracewing, 2005.

Shrimpton, Paul. *The "Making of Men": The Idea and Reality of Newman's University in Oxford and Dublin*. Gracewing, 2014.

Tristram, Henry, ed. *John Henry Newman: Autobiographical Writings*. Sheed and Ward, 1956.

Turner, Frank M. Introduction to *Apologia Pro Vita Sua and Six Sermons.* Yale University Press, 2008.

Ward, Maisie. *Young Mr. Newman.* Sheed and Ward, 1948.

Ward, Wilfrid Philip. *The Life of John Henry Cardinal Newman.* 2 vols. Longmans, Green and Co., 1912.

Wiseman, Nicholas. "The Anglican Claim," *Dublin Review,* July 1839.

Roman Pontiffs:

Benedict XVI. "Address to the Bishops of the Episcopal Conference of England and Wales on Their 'Ad Limina' Visit." February 1, 2010.

Benedict XVI. General Audience. St. Peter's Square. June 16, 2010.

Benedict XVI. Angelus. Cofton Park of Rednal, Birmingham. September 19, 2010.

Benedict XVI. Interview with the Journalists During the Flight to the United Kingdom. Apostolic Journey to the United Kingdom. September 16, 2010.

Benedict XVI. "Address During Visit to the Archbishop of Canterbury." Lambeth Palace. September 17, 2010.

Benedict XVI. "Address at Prayer Vigil on the Eve of the Beatification of Cardinal John Henry Newman." Hyde Park, London. September 18, 2010.

Benedict XVI. General Audience. Saint Peter's Square. September 22, 2010.

Benedict XVI. "Message on the Occasion of the Symposium Organized by the International Centre of Newman Friends." November 18, 2010.

Benedict XVI. "Address to Members of the International Theological Commission." Consistory Hall. December 3, 2010.

Benedict XVI. "Address on the Occasion of Christmas Greetings to the Roman Curia." Sala Regia. December 20, 2010.

Benedict XVI. "Homily at Papal Mass for the Episcopal Ordination of Five Archbishops." Vatican Basilica. February 5, 2011.

Benedict XVI. "Address to H. E. Mr. Nigel Marcus Baker, New Ambassador of the United Kingdom of Great Britain and Northern Ireland to the Holy See." Apostolic Palace, Castel Gandolfo. September 9, 2011.

Benedict XVI. "Address to Participants in the World Congress for the Pastoral Care of International Students." Consistory Hall. December 2, 2011.

Benedict XVI. "Social Networks: Portals of Truth and Faith; New Spaces for Evangelization." Message for the 47th World Communications Day, May 12, 2013.

Francis. Encyclical Letter on Faith *Lumen Fidei*. June 29, 2013.

Francis. Apostolic Exhortation on the Proclamation of the Gospel in Today's World *Evangelii Gaudium*. November 24, 2013.

Francis. *My Door Is Always Open: A Conversation on Faith, Hope and the Church in a Time of Change*. Bloomsbury Continuum, 2014.

Francis. "Video Message of His Holiness Pope Francis to Participants in the 3rd International Symposium on the Apostolic Exhortation 'Amoris Laetitia.'" November 11, 2017.

Francis. Apostolic Constitution on Ecclesiastical Universities and Faculties *Veritatis Gaudium*. January 29, 2018.

Francis. "Homily at Holy Mass and Canonization of the Blesseds: John Henry Newman, Giuseppina Vannini, Mariam Thresia Chiramel Mankidiyan, Dulce Lopes Pontes, Marguerite Bays." St. Peter's Square. October 13, 2019.

Francis. "Address to Rectors, Professors, Students and Staff of the Roman Pontifical Universities and Institutions." Paul VI Audience Hall. February 25, 2023.

Francis. Encyclical Letter on the Human and Divine Love of the Heart of Jesus Christ *Dilexit Nos*. October 24, 2024.

John Paul II. "Letter to the Archbishop of Birmingham for the Centenary of the Elevation to the Cardinalate of John Henry Newman." April 7, 1979.

John Paul II. "Address to the Participants in the Academic Symposium Organized to Commemorate the Centenary of the Death of Cardinal John Henry Newman." April 27, 1990.

John Paul II. "Letter to the Archbishop of Birmingham on the First Centenary of the Death of John Henry Newman." June 18, 1990.

John Paul II, Encyclical Letter *Veritas Splendor*. August 6, 1993.

John Paul II. "Letter on the Occasion of the 2nd Centenary of the Birth of Cardinal John Henry Newman." January 22, 2001.

John XIII. Encyclical Letter on Truth, Unity and Peace *Ad Petri Cathedram*. June 29, 1959.

Paul VI. *Discorso di Paolo VI ai Pellegrini Convenuti per la Beatificazione di Domenico della Madre di Dio* (Homily for the Beatification of Bl. Dominic of the Mother of God). October 27, 1963.

Paul VI. "The Wealth of Cardinal Newman's Thought." Address to Newman Congress, May 17, 1970. *L'Osservatore Romano* (English edition), June 4, 1970, 114. Newman Reader. https://www.newmanreader.org/canonization/popes/or4jun70.html.

Paul VI. "Address to the Participants in the Cardinal Newman Academic Symposium." April 7, 1974.

Paul VI. "Address to a Group of Bishops from England on their 'Ad Limina' Visit." November 10, 1977.

Pius IX. Papal Bull *Universalis Ecclesiae*. September 29, 1850.

Pius IX. Apostolic Constitution on the Immaculate Conception *Ineffabilis Deus*. December 8, 1854.

Pius X. Encyclical Letter on the Doctrines of the Modernists *Pascendi Dominici* Gregis. September 8, 1907.

Pius XII. "The Service of Truth." Letter to the Archbishop of Westminster for the Newman Centenary. *The Tablet*, October 13, 1945. Newman Reader. https://www.newmanreader.org/canonization/popes/tablet13oct45.html

About the Author

Msgr. Laurence Spiteri is a priest of the Archdiocese of Los Angeles, California, and serves as Prelate Auditor of the Roman Rota at the Vatican and Commissioner of ratum et non consummatum cases. He holds doctorates in biblical studies, psychology, and canon law with a specialization in international law regarding the Church-state relationship. He serves as the official in charge of the Legal Office of the Vatican Apostolic Library, a voting member of the Historical Commission of the Dicastery of the Causes of Saints, an ad hoc judge at the Dicastery for the Doctrine of the Faith, a consultant to various Roman dicasteries and religious communities, and CEO of the Sanctuary of Culture Foundation, the Treasures of History Foundation, and the St. Joseph, Husband of Mary Foundation. He is a former Associate Director and Judge at the Metropolitan Tribunal of Los Angeles, Judge at the Tribunal of Las Vegas, assistant at the Apostolic Signatura, instructor in canonical procedures, and visiting professor of Sacred Scripture, Church History, History of Medieval Philosophy, and Catholic Theology in various academic institutions. He is the author of ninety-six books, some of which deal with canon and civil law, as well as ninety-three articles that appear in various professional publications. He has been published in various languages in the United States, England, Ireland, Malta, Mexico, Portugal, Italy, and Vatican City State.

Sophia Institute

Sophia Institute is a nonprofit institution that seeks to nurture the spiritual, moral, and cultural life of souls and to spread the gospel of Christ in conformity with the authentic teachings of the Roman Catholic Church.

Sophia Institute Press fulfills this mission by offering translations, reprints, and new publications that afford readers a rich source of the enduring wisdom of mankind.

Sophia Institute also operates the popular online resource CatholicExchange.com. *Catholic Exchange* provides world news from a Catholic perspective as well as daily devotionals and articles that will help readers to grow in holiness and live a life consistent with the teachings of the Church.

In 2013, Sophia Institute launched Sophia Institute for Teachers to renew and rebuild Catholic culture through service to Catholic education. With the goal of nurturing the spiritual, moral, and cultural life of souls, and an abiding respect for the role and work of teachers, we strive to provide materials and programs that are at once enlightening to the mind and ennobling to the heart; faithful and complete, as well as useful and practical.

Sophia Institute gratefully recognizes the Solidarity Association for preserving and encouraging the growth of our apostolate over the course of many years. Without their generous and timely support, this book would not be in your hands.

www.SophiaInstitute.com
www.CatholicExchange.com
www.SophiaTeachers.org

Sophia Institute Press is a registered trademark of Sophia Institute.
Sophia Institute is a tax-exempt institution as defined by the
Internal Revenue Code, Section 501(c)(3). Tax ID 22-2548708.